THE AUSTRALIAN
Women's Weekly
Moroccan

acp
books

contents

moroccan essentials

Morocco, in the vibrant north-western corner of Africa, is home to one of the world's most diversified cuisines. It is the harmony of flavours, the perfect balance of savoury and sweet, fused with elaborate spices, that creates the rich complexity unique to Moroccan food. To experience true Moroccan food is to connect with its past and to feel a sense of continuity with its rich history. Morocco's culinary traditions are a reflection of the indigenous Berber culture and strong Arab, Middle-Eastern, Persian and Andalusian influences that have reigned at various stages of Morocco's history. This combination of cultural influences has created the magical and exciting fusion of flavours that is Moroccan food.

Food is seen as much more than just sustenance in Morocco. There are few places where food is more lovingly and artistically prepared, more delightfully presented, and more thoroughly enjoyed. Moroccan hospitality is legendary – when entering a Moroccan home you are offered food and tea within a heartbeat. A Moroccan diffa, or banquet, is an abundance of riches generously shared that honours friends, family and visitors, and is a great source of pride to the host.

Moroccans, in the tradition of the Arabs, eat with the first three fingers of their right hands. Before dining they go through an elaborate hand-washing process, whereby a servant or young member of the family brings water, a basin and a hand towel to the table. The main meal of the day is usually served at midday, and begins with a series of hot and cold salads, followed by a tagine, or sometimes a succession of tagines, and an enormous platter of couscous. Bread, called kisra or khboz, is very important in Moroccan cuisine and is eaten with every meal. Moroccan bread is round, heavy-textured and spicy. It is highly absorbent and ideal for soaking up the sauces of tagines, and also acts as a kind of utensil to scoop up the food. Meals are traditionally finished with a bowl or tray of fruits and nuts, and always a glass of simple, soothing, sweet mint tea.

Food in Morocco also has significant religious importance, and certain dishes are eaten in relation to the religious calendar. Being a predominantly Islamic country, pork and alcohol are not consumed. Couscous is traditionally served for lunch on Friday, the Islamic holy day, although it is also eaten at numerous other occasions, especially feasts or any special occasions. During Ramadan, the holy month of fasting, not a bite of food or drop of water is consumed between sunrise and sunset. The fast is traditionally broken at sundown with a thick, hearty bowl of harira soup followed by dates, honey cake and milk or coffee. Bread is thought to be sacred and is treated with utmost respect. If a piece is seen lying on the ground, someone will pick it up, kiss it, and thank Allah for the gift of bread.

couscous

Couscous is often thought of as the crowning achievement of Moroccan cuisine. Simple but brilliant, these hand-rolled grains of golden semolina are steamed above a simmering tagine until they swell and become soft and fluffy, flavoured by the tagine.

tagines

Tagine refers to the name of the unique Moroccan cooking pot as well as the wonderful rich stews that are cooked within it. The traditional tagine pot is made of clay and consists of two parts – the flat round base with low sides, and the tall cone-shaped lid. The base of the tagine serves as both a cooking and serving dish, while the lid acts like a closed chimney, trapping in the moisture and circulating the steam and flavours in the pot during cooking. Traditionally tagines would be cooked over coals or an open flame, but you can use tagines at home over a gas flame, on an electric stove or in the oven. When cooking with a tagine at home, follow the manufacturer's instructions.

Tagine recipes are aromatic and flavoursome, almost always made with meat, vegetables and a medley of other ingredients and exotic spices. One unique characteristic of some tagines is the blend of sweet and savoury. Prunes, raisins, quinces, honey and dates are frequently found alongside beef, lamb, chicken and vegetables, skilfully fused to create complex, distinctive and delicious dishes. The secret to success with tagines is to simmer them gently for hours, until the meat is meltingly tender and the rich aroma of beautiful spices escapes the pot and seduces you to the table.

drinks & snacks

citrus sparkler

⅔ cup (160ml) each strained lemon, orange and
  ruby red grapefruit juice
½ cup (110g) caster (superfine) sugar
½ teaspoon orange blossom water
1 small ruby red grapefruit (350g), quartered,
  sliced thinly
½ cup loosely packed fresh mint leaves
5 cups (1.25 litres) chilled sparkling mineral water

1   Stir juices and sugar in large jug until sugar
dissolves. Stir in remaining ingredients.
2   Serve over ice.

prep time 20 minutes **makes** 6 cups (1.5 litres)
nutritional count per 1 cup (250ml) 0.2g total fat
(0g saturated fat); 451kJ (108 cal);
25g carbohydrate; 0.9g protein; 0.6g fibre

chilli spiced olives

1½ cups (240g) mixed rainbow olives
1 tablespoon each lemon and orange juice
1 tablespoon olive oil
2 tablespoons finely chopped fresh flat-leaf parsley
2 teaspoons finely chopped preserved lemon rind
1 teaspoon harissa paste
½ teaspoon each ground cumin and sweet paprika
¼ teaspoon white sugar
1 clove garlic, crushed

1   Combine ingredients in medium bowl. Cover,
refrigerate 2 hours.

prep time 10 minutes (+ refrigeration) **serves** 4
nutritional count per serving 6.1g total fat
(0.8g saturated fat); 414kJ (99 cal);
9.7g carbohydrate; 0.6g protein; 1.7g fibre

note Preserved lemon is available at delis and
some supermarkets. Remove and discard the flesh,
rinse the rind, then use it as the recipe directs.

mint tea

5 cups (1.25 litres) boiling water
1 cup firmly packed fresh mint leaves
¼ cup (55g) raw sugar
15g (½ ounce) green tea leaves

1 Combine 1 cup of the water and ⅔ cup mint in medium heatproof jug; drain, reserve mint.
2 Combine the drained mint with the remaining water, sugar and tea in medium saucepan; stir over heat until sugar dissolves. Bring to the boil.
3 Strain tea into large heatproof jug.
4 Serve cups of tea topped with remaining mint.

prep + cook time 15 minutes **makes** 4 cups (1 litre)
nutritional count per 1 cup (250ml) 0.1g total fat (0g saturated fat); 247kJ (59 cal);
14.3g carbohydrate; 0.4g protein; 0.9g fibre

notes Blanching the mint leaves in boiling water in step 1 removes any bitterness. You will need about nine green tea bags for this recipe.

almond milk

2 cups (320g) blanched almonds
2 cups (500ml) buttermilk
2 cups (500ml) milk
⅓ cup (75g) caster (superfine) sugar
½ teaspoon orange blossom water
pinch nutmeg

1 Blend nuts, buttermilk and half the milk until smooth.
2 Stir remaining milk and sugar in small saucepan over heat until sugar dissolves. Cool.
3 Combine almond mixture and milk mixture in large jug; stir in orange blossom water. Refrigerate 3 hours or until required.
4 Serve almond milk over ice; sprinkle with nutmeg.

prep + cook time 20 minutes (+ refrigeration)
makes 6 cups (1.5 litres)
nutritional count per 1 cup (250ml) 34.6g total fat (5g saturated fat); 1994kJ (477 cal);
23.3g carbohydrate; 17.4g protein; 4.7g fibre

green apple and rosewater milk

4 medium green-skinned apples (600g), peeled, cored, chopped coarsely
½ teaspoon rosewater
2 cups (500ml) milk
2 tablespoons caster (superfine) sugar

1 Process ingredients until smooth.
2 Strain mixture into large jug; serve over ice.

prep time 15 minutes **makes** 4 cups (1 litre)
nutritional count per 1 cup (250ml) 5g total fat
(3.2g saturated fat); 727kJ (174 cal);
27.6g carbohydrate; 4.6g protein; 2.3g fibre

spiced coffee with rosewater cream

8 cardamom pods
3 cinnamon sticks
4 cloves
¾ cup (30g) instant coffee granules
1 litre (4 cups) water
¼ cup (55g) light brown sugar
⅓ cup (80ml) pouring cream
1 teaspoon rosewater

1 Dry-fry spices in small frying pan until fragrant.
2 Combine spices, coffee, the water and sugar in medium saucepan; stir over heat until sugar dissolves. Bring to the boil. Reduce heat; simmer, stirring occasionally, 10 minutes.
3 Meanwhile, beat cream and rosewater in small bowl with electric mixer until soft peaks form.
4 Strain hot coffee into serving cups; serve topped with rosewater cream.

prep + cook time 15 minutes **makes** 4 cups (1 litre)
nutritional count per 1 cup (250ml) 8.7g total fat
(5.7g saturated fat); 589kJ (141 cal);
14.6g carbohydrate; 1.4g protein; 1.2g fibre

vegetarian cigars with harissa yogurt

1 medium red capsicum (bell pepper) (200g)
1 tablespoon olive oil
1 clove garlic, crushed
1 small eggplant (230g), chopped finely
1 large zucchini (150g), chopped finely
1 large tomato (220g), seeded, chopped finely
1 teaspoon each ground cumin and sweet paprika
1 tablespoon finely chopped fresh mint
6 sheets fillo pastry
75g (2½ ounces) butter, melted
HARISSA YOGURT
½ cup (140g) yogurt
1 teaspoon harissa paste
1 teaspoon finely grated lemon rind

1 Preheat oven to 200°C/400°F. Oil oven trays.
2 Quarter capsicum; discard seeds and membranes. Roast, skin-side up, until skin blisters and blackens. Cover capsicum with plastic or paper for 5 minutes; peel away skin, then chop capsicum finely.
3 Meanwhile, heat oil in large frying pan; stir garlic, eggplant, zucchini and tomato about 5 minutes or until vegetables soften. Add spices; cook, stirring, about 5 minutes or until fragrant. Stir in capsicum and mint; cool. Season to taste.
4 Brush 1 sheet of pastry with butter; top with a second pastry sheet. Cut layered sheets lengthways into 3 rectangles. Halve pastry rectangles crossways. Press 1 tablespoon of vegetable mixture into a log shape along one short end of each rectangle. Roll pastry over filling; fold in sides then roll up to form a cigar shape. Repeat to make a total of 18 cigars.
5 Place cigars, seam-side down, on oven trays; brush with remaining butter. Bake about 20 minutes or until browned lightly.
6 Meanwhile, make harissa yogurt; serve with cigars.
HARISSA YOGURT Combine ingredients in small bowl.

prep + cook time 55 minutes makes 18
nutritional count per cigar 4.8g total fat
(2.5g saturated fat); 276kJ (66 cal);
4g carbohydrate; 1.3g protein; 0.8g fibre

zaalouk (eggplant dip)

2 large eggplants (1kg)
½ cup (125ml) olive oil
6 medium tomatoes (900g)
3 cloves garlic, crushed
⅓ cup each coarsely chopped fresh flat-leaf
  parsley and coriander (cilantro)
1 teaspoon ground cumin

1 Preheat oven to 200°C/400°F.
2 Pierce eggplants all over with fork or skewer.
Place eggplants on oiled oven tray; drizzle with
2 tablespoons of the oil. Roast eggplants,
uncovered, about 50 minutes or until softened.
3 Meanwhile, place tomatoes on another oiled
oven tray; drizzle with 2 tablespoons of the oil.
Roast tomatoes for last 15 minutes of eggplant
cooking time. Cool 20 minutes.

4 When cool enough to handle, peel eggplants
and tomatoes; discard skin. Seed tomatoes; chop
tomato and eggplant flesh coarsely.
5 Heat remaining oil in large frying pan; cook garlic,
eggplant and tomato, stirring occasionally, about
20 minutes or until thick. Add herbs; cook, stirring,
5 minutes. Transfer mixture to medium bowl, stir in
cumin; cool 20 minutes. Season to taste.

prep + cook time 1 hour 20 minutes (+ cooling)
makes 3 cups
nutritional count per tablespoon 3.3g total fat
(0.5g saturated fat); 150kJ (36 cal);
0.9g carbohydrate; 0.4g protein; 0.8g fibre

Serve with crusty bread.

krachel (sweet moroccan rolls)

1½ tablespoons dried yeast
¼ cup (60ml) warm water
½ cup (110g) caster (superfine) sugar
2 cups (300g) plain (all-purpose) flour
2 tablespoons sesame seeds
3 teaspoons anise seeds
¼ cup (60ml) milk
60g (2 ounces) butter, melted
1 egg
1 tablespoon orange blossom water
1 egg yolk
2 teaspoons sesame seeds, extra

1 Combine yeast, the water and 2 teaspoons of the sugar in small heatproof bowl, cover; stand in a warm place about 10 minutes or until mixture is frothy.
2 Combine sifted flour, remaining sugar and seeds in large bowl. Stir in yeast mixture, milk, butter, egg and orange blossom water. Knead dough on floured surface about 10 minutes or until smooth and elastic. Place dough in oiled medium bowl, cover; stand in warm place about 1 hour or until doubled in size.
3 Preheat oven to 180°C/350°F. Oil oven trays.
4 Divide dough into 12 pieces; roll each piece into a ball. Place balls, about 5cm (2 inches) apart, on oven trays; cover loosely with oiled plastic wrap. Stand in warm place 20 minutes.
5 Discard plastic wrap. Brush balls with egg yolk, sprinkle with extra sesame seeds. Bake about 20 minutes.

prep + cook time 50 minutes (+ standing)
makes 12
nutritional count per roll 6.8g total fat (3.3g saturated fat); 798kJ (191 cal); 27.5g carbohydrate; 4.6g protein; 1.2g fibre

note Krachel are sweet, fragrant rolls flavoured with anise seeds, sesame seeds and orange flower water. They are perfect served warm, with butter, for morning or afternoon tea.

minted tuna triangles

1 tablespoon olive oil
1 medium brown onion (150g), chopped finely
4 drained anchovy fillets, chopped finely
2 teaspoons ground cumin
425g (12 ounces) canned tuna in brine,
   drained, flaked
1 egg, beaten lightly
⅓ cup finely chopped fresh flat-leaf parsley
¼ cup finely chopped fresh mint
12 sheets fillo pastry
90g (3 ounces) butter, melted
2 teaspoons poppy seeds

1   Heat oil in large frying pan; cook onion and
anchovy, stirring, about 5 minutes or until soft.
Add cumin, tuna, egg, parsley and mint; cook,
stirring, about 30 seconds or until egg starts to
set. Remove from heat, season to taste; cool.
2   Preheat oven to 200°C/400°F. Oil oven trays;
line with baking paper.
3   Brush 1 sheet of pastry with butter; top with
two more sheets, brushing each with butter. Cut
layered sheets crossways into 5 strips. Place
1 rounded tablespoon of tuna mixture at one
short end of each pastry strip. Fold one corner
of pastry diagonally over filling to form a triangle.
Continue folding to end of strip, retaining triangle
shape. Repeat to make a total of 20 triangles.
4   Place triangles on trays; brush with remaining
butter, sprinkle with poppy seeds. Bake triangles
about 20 minutes or until browned lightly.

prep + cook time 55 minutes **makes** 20
nutritional count per triangle 5.7g total fat
(2.9g saturated fat); 393kJ (94 cal);
5.1g carbohydrate; 5.4g protein; 0.4g fibre

Serve with yogurt and lemon wedges.

chilli, cumin and garlic prawns

1kg (2 pounds) uncooked medium king prawns
¼ cup (60ml) olive oil
3 cloves garlic, sliced thinly
1 fresh long red chilli, sliced thinly
2.5cm (1 inch) piece fresh ginger (15g),
  cut into matchsticks
1 teaspoon each cumin seeds and sweet paprika
¼ cup each loosely packed fresh flat-leaf parsley
  and coriander (cilantro) leaves

1   Shell and devein prawns, leaving tails intact.
2   Heat oil in large frying pan; stir garlic, chilli,
ginger and spices about 2 minutes or until fragrant.
Add prawns; cook, stirring, about 5 minutes or until
prawns are changed in colour. Season to taste.
3   Serve prawns sprinkled with herbs; accompany
with lemon wedges.

prep + cook time 40 minutes **serves** 6 as a starter
nutritional count per serving 9.7g total fat
(1.4g saturated fat); 660kJ (158 cal);
0.3g carbohydrate; 17.3g protein; 0.5g fibre

briwat (lamb fillo cigars)

1 tablespoon olive oil
1 medium brown onion (150g), chopped finely
2 cloves garlic, crushed
500g minced (ground) lamb
1 teaspoon each ground cumin, cinnamon, ginger
  and coriander
2 tablespoons roasted slivered almonds
1 teaspoon finely grated lemon rind
1 tablespoon lemon juice
⅓ cup finely chopped fresh coriander (cilantro)
18 sheets fillo pastry
155g (5 ounces) butter, melted
½ cup (140g) yogurt

1 Heat oil in large frying pan; stir onion and garlic, until onion softens. Add mince and spices; cook, stirring, until mince is browned. Stir in nuts, rind, juice and half the coriander; cool. Season to taste.
2 Preheat oven to 200°C/400°F. Grease and line oven trays.
3 Brush 1 sheet of pastry with butter; top with 2 more sheets, brushing each with butter. Cut layered sheets lengthways into 3 rectangles. Press a rounded tablespoon of lamb mixture into a log shape along one short end of each rectangle. Roll pastry over filling; fold in sides then roll up to make a cigar shape. Repeat to make a total of 18 cigars.
4 Place cigars, seam-side down, on oven trays; brush with remaining butter. Bake about 15 minutes or until browned lightly.
5 Meanwhile, combine yogurt and remaining coriander in small bowl; accompany cigars with yogurt and lemon wedges.

prep + cook time 1 hour **makes** 18
nutritional count per briwat 11.6g total fat (6.3g saturated fat); 715kJ (171 cal); 8.7g carbohydrate; 7.8g protein; 0.6g fibre

slada felfla (capsicum dip)

4 large red capsicums (bell peppers) (1.4kg)
3 cloves garlic, unpeeled
2 tablespoons olive oil
1 tablespoon red wine vinegar
1 tablespoon lemon juice
1 tablespoon finely chopped preserved lemon rind
½ teaspoon hot paprika
2 tablespoons finely chopped fresh coriander
  (cilantro)

1 Preheat oven to 220°C/425°F. Oil oven trays.
2 Quarter capsicums; discard seeds and membranes.
Roast, skin-side up, with garlic about 30 minutes or
until skin blisters and blackens. Cover capsicum
and garlic with plastic or paper for 5 minutes, then
peel away skins.
3 Blend or process capsicum, garlic, oil, vinegar,
juice, preserved lemon and paprika until smooth.
Stir in coriander; season to taste.

prep + cook time 45 minutes **makes** 1½ cups
nutritional count per tablespoon 2.2g total fat
(0.3g saturated fat); 155kJ (37 cal);
2.7g carbohydrate; 1.1g protein; 0.9g fibre

Serve dip with crusty bread; we used toasted
pitta bread.

goat's cheese with chickpeas and capsicum

2 large green capsicums (bell peppers) (700g)
2 large red capsicums (bell peppers) (700g)
2 tablespoons olive oil
1 medium red onion (170g), sliced thinly
2 cloves garlic, crushed
1 teaspoon ground cumin
½ teaspoon hot paprika
400g (15 ounces) canned chickpeas
   (garbanzo beans), rinsed, drained
2 teaspoons finely grated lemon rind
1 tablespoon lemon juice
⅓ cup coarsely chopped fresh flat-leaf parsley
60g (2 ounces) soft goat's cheese

1   Preheat oven to 200°C/400°F. Oil oven trays.
2   Quarter capsicums; discard seeds and membranes. Roast, skin-side up, until skin blisters and blackens. Cover capsicum with plastic or paper for 5 minutes; peel away skin, then slice capsicum thinly.
3   Heat oil in large frying pan; stir onion and garlic, until onion softens. Add spices and half the chickpeas; cook, stirring, about 2 minutes or until fragrant. Add capsicum; cook, stirring, until heated through. Remove from heat; stir in rind, juice and parsley. Cool.
4   Meanwhile, coarsely mash remaining chickpeas with cheese in medium bowl.
5   Stir capsicum mixture into cheese mixture; season to taste.

prep + cook time 50 minutes **makes** 3 cups
nutritional count per tablespoon 1.5g total fat
(0.3g saturated fat); 121kJ (29 cal);
2.3g carbohydrate; 1.3g protein; 0.8g fibre

Serve dip with bread; we used soft rolls, but a toasted pitta bread would go just as well.

hummus

800g (30 ounces) canned chickpeas
   (garbanzo beans), rinsed, drained
¼ cup (90g) honey
¼ cup (60ml) lemon juice
¼ cup (60ml) olive oil
4cm (1½ inch) piece fresh turmeric (20g), grated
2 cloves garlic, crushed
1 teaspoon ground cumin
¼ teaspoon cayenne pepper
1 tablespoon finely chopped fresh coriander
   (cilantro)

1 Blend or process chickpeas, honey, juice, half
the oil, turmeric, garlic, cumin and half the cayenne
pepper until smooth. Transfer mixture to medium
bowl; stir in coriander, season to taste.
2 Serve hummus sprinkled with remaining cayenne
pepper and drizzled with remaining oil.

prep time 10 minutes **makes** 2 cups
nutritional count per tablespoon 2.7g total fat
(0.4g saturated fat); 234kJ (56 cal);
6.2g carbohydrate; 1.4g protein; 1.1g fibre

Serve dip with crusty bread; we used toasted
pitta bread.

chickpea and silver beet salad

8 spring onions (200g)
600g (1¼ pounds) canned chickpeas
  (garbanzo beans), rinsed, drained
1kg silver beet (swiss chard), trimmed,
  shredded finely
1 large red capsicum (bell pepper) (350g),
  sliced thinly
PAPRIKA DRESSING
⅓ cup (80ml) mustard seed oil
2 teaspoons sweet paprika
1 tablespoon lemon juice
1 tablespoon light brown sugar

1 Make paprika dressing.
2 Trim green tops from spring onion bulbs. Cut
bulbs into wedges; thinly slice three of the green
tops, discard remaining tops.
3 Combine onions with remaining ingredients and
three-quarters of the dressing in large bowl; season
to taste.
4 Serve salad drizzled with remaining dressing.
PAPRIKA DRESSING Combine ingredients in
screw-top jar; shake well.

prep time 20 minutes **serves** 6
nutritional count per serving 13.9g total fat
(1.7g saturated fat); 882kJ (211 cal);
14.2g carbohydrate; 5.8g protein; 4.7g fibre

notes Mustard seed oil can be found in most large
supermarkets or health-food stores.
A 1kg bunch of silver beet should give you about
250g after trimming.

salads

cucumber and fetta salad with za'atar

2 lebanese cucumbers (260g), peeled, sliced thinly
90g (3 ounces) goat's milk fetta cheese
2 tablespoons finely chopped fresh mint
1 tablespoon lemon juice
1 tablespoon olive oil
2 teaspoons za'atar

1 Arrange cucumber on large serving platter.
2 Combine cheese and mint in small bowl; sprinkle cheese mixture over cucumber. Drizzle with juice and oil, then sprinkle with za'atar.

prep time 10 minutes **serves** 4
nutritional count per serving 9.9g total fat
(4.1g saturated fat); 468kJ (112 cal);
1.2g carbohydrate; 4.3g protein; 0.7g fibre

note Za'atar is a Middle-Eastern blend of whole roasted sesame seeds, sumac and crushed dried herbs such as wild marjoram and thyme, although its content is largely determined by the individual maker. It is available from some large supermarkets, delicatessens and Middle-Eastern food stores. Replace it with dried oregano if unavailable.

23

sweet cucumber and orange salad

2 large oranges (600g)
1 telegraph (hothouse) cucumber (400g)
2 cups loosely packed fresh mint leaves
HONEY LEMON DRESSING
¼ cup (60ml) avocado oil
1 tablespoon finely grated lemon rind
1 tablespoon lemon juice
2 teaspoons honey

1 Make honey lemon dressing.
2 Segment oranges over small bowl; reserve juice.
3 Use vegetable peeler to cut cucumber into thin ribbons. Combine cucumber, mint, orange segments, reserved orange juice and dressing in medium bowl; season to taste.
HONEY LEMON DRESSING Combine ingredients in screw-top jar; shake well.

prep time 20 minutes serves 4
nutritional count per serving 14.3g total fat (1.7g saturated fat); 840kJ (201 cal); 13.5g carbohydrate; 2.6g protein; 4.6g fibre

note Traditionally served as an accompaniment to spicy dishes, this recipe would also make a great light vegetarian starter.

salad of herbs

60g (2 ounces) baby rocket (arugula)
½ cup each loosely packed fresh flat-leaf parsley
  and coriander (cilantro) leaves
2 cups (230g) firmly packed trimmed watercress
½ small red onion (50g), sliced thinly
⅓ cup (55g) seeded mixed olives, chopped coarsely
PRESERVED LEMON DRESSING
1 clove garlic, crushed
1 tablespoon olive oil
¼ teaspoon sweet paprika
2 tablespoons lemon juice
1 tablespoon finely chopped preserved lemon rind

1   Make preserved lemon dressing.
2   Combine ingredients and dressing in large bowl; season to taste.
PRESERVED LEMON DRESSING Combine ingredients in screw-top jar; shake well.

prep time 15 minutes **serves** 4
nutritional count per serving 5.3g total fat (0.7g saturated fat); 339kJ (81 cal); 3.9g carbohydrate; 2.6g protein; 3.5g fibre

roasted capsicum and beetroot salad

500g (1 pound) baby beetroot (beets)
1 small red, orange and yellow capsicums
  (bell pepper) (150g each)
cooking-oil spray
½ small red onion (50g), chopped finely
1 tablespoon finely chopped fresh flat-leaf parsley
1 tablespoon thinly sliced preserved lemon rind
1 tablespoon lemon juice

1 Preheat oven to 220°C/425°F.
2 Trim leaves from beetroot; wrap each beetroot in foil, place on oven tray. Place capsicums on baking (parchment) paper lined oven tray; spray with oil. Roast beetroot and capsicums about 30 minutes or until beetroot are tender and capsicums have blistered and blackened.
3 Cool beetroot 10 minutes then peel and quarter. Cover capsicums with plastic or paper for 5 minutes. Quarter capsicums; discard seeds and membranes. Peel away skin, then halve each quarter lengthways.
4 Arrange beetroot and capsicum on large serving platter. Sprinkle with onion, parsley and preserved lemon; drizzle with juice.

prep + cook time 50 minutes **serves** 4
nutritional count per serving 1.6g total fat
(0.2g saturated fat); 397kJ (95 cal);
13.9g carbohydrate; 3.9g protein; 4.8g fibre

spicy lentil and rice salad

1 cup (200g) basmati rice
¼ cup (60ml) olive oil
30g (1 ounce) butter
4 medium red onions (680g), sliced thinly
4 cloves garlic, crushed
2 teaspoons each ground cinnamon, coriander, cumin and sweet paprika
4 green onions (scallions), sliced thinly
400g (14 ounces) canned brown lentils, rinsed, drained

1 Cook rice in medium saucepan of boiling water until tender; drain. Rinse under cold water; drain.
2 Meanwhile, heat oil and butter in large frying pan; cook red onion and garlic, stirring occasionally, about 20 minutes or until onion is lightly caramelised.
3 Add spices; cook, stirring, about 1 minute or until fragrant.
4 Remove from heat; stir in green onion, lentils and rice. Season to taste. Serve warm.

prep + cook time 35 minutes **serves** 6
nutritional count per serving 13.7g total fat (4g saturated fat); 1258kJ (301 cal); 37.3g carbohydrate; 5.9g protein; 3.5g fibre

tomato and preserved lemon salad

750g (1½ pounds) baby egg (plum) truss
  tomatoes, halved
1 small red onion (100g), sliced thinly
½ cup firmly packed fresh coriander (cilantro) leaves
PRESERVED LEMON DRESSING
⅓ cup (80ml) lemon juice
2 tablespoons olive oil
1 tablespoon finely chopped preserved lemon rind
1 tablespoon finely chopped fresh flat-leaf parsley
1 clove garlic, crushed
½ teaspoon white sugar
¼ teaspoon ground cumin
pinch sweet paprika

1   Make preserved lemon dressing.
2   Combine tomato, onion, coriander and
dressing in large bowl; season to taste.
PRESERVED LEMON DRESSING Combine
ingredients in screw-top jar; shake well.

prep time 10 minutes **serves** 6
nutritional count per serving 6.3g total fat
(0.9g saturated fat); 355kJ (85 cal);
4.5g carbohydrate; 1g protein; 2.4g fibre

carrot, raisin and herb salad

1.2kg (2½ pounds) baby carrots, trimmed
¼ cup (60ml) olive oil
1 teaspoon each ground cumin and sweet paprika
½ teaspoon ground cinnamon
¼ cup (60ml) orange juice
2 tablespoons lemon juice
⅓ cup (50g) raisins
⅔ cup coarsely chopped fresh flat-leaf parsley
¼ cup firmly packed fresh mint leaves

1 Preheat oven to 200°C/400°F.
2 Combine carrots, half the oil and spices in large shallow baking dish; roast, uncovered, about 15 minutes or until carrots are tender. Cool 20 minutes.
3 Meanwhile, make dressing by combining juices, raisins, remaining oil and half the parsley in large jug; season to taste.
4 Serve carrots drizzled with dressing; sprinkle with mint and remaining parsley.

prep + cook time 30 minutes (+ cooling) **serves** 6
nutritional count per serving 9.4g total fat (1.3g saturated fat); 698kJ (167 cal); 16.2g carbohydrate; 1.9g protein; 5.9g fibre

note You need 3 bunches of baby carrots, also known as dutch carrots; they're available from supermarkets and greengrocers.

eggplant and tomato salad

6 baby eggplants (360g)
¼ cup (60ml) olive oil
½ teaspoon each ground cumin, coriander and
  smoked paprika
1 medium tomato (150g), seeded, chopped finely
1 small red onion (100g), chopped finely
2 tablespoons (20g) seeded black olives,
  chopped finely
1 tablespoon finely chopped fresh flat-leaf parsley
2 teaspoons finely chopped fresh mint
1 teaspoon finely grated lemon rind
2 teaspoons lemon juice

1 Carefully cut eggplants lengthways into four
slices, leaving tops intact. Combine eggplant and
half the oil in medium bowl; season.
2 Cook eggplants on heated oiled grill plate (or
grill or barbecue), flattening and fanning with the
back of a spatula, until eggplants are tender.
3 Meanwhile, dry-fry spices in small frying pan
until fragrant; cool. Combine spices, remaining oil
and remaining ingredients in small bowl; season.
4 Serve eggplant; drizzled with tomato mixture.

prep + cook time 35 minutes **serves** 6
nutritional count per serving 9.3g total fat
(1.3g saturated fat); 435kJ (104 cal);
3.3g carbohydrate; 1.1g protein; 1.8g fibre

orange and radish salad

4 medium oranges (960g)
500g (1 pound) red radishes, trimmed
1 tablespoon olive oil
2 teaspoons white wine vinegar
¼ cup finely chopped fresh mint

1 Finely grate 2 teaspoons rind from half an orange. Segment oranges over small bowl; reserve 1 tablespoon juice.
2 Using mandolin or V-slicer, slice radishes as thinly as possible.
3 Whisk reserved juice, oil and vinegar in medium bowl. Add rind, orange segments, radish and mint; toss gently. Serve immediately.

prep + cook time 25 minutes **serves** 4
nutritional count per serving 5g total fat
(0.6g saturated fat); 535kJ (128 cal);
15.6g carbohydrate; 2.7g protein; 4.8g fibre

notes You need a bunch of red radishes for this recipe.
This recipe is best made just before serving; it will become soggy if left standing.

couscous

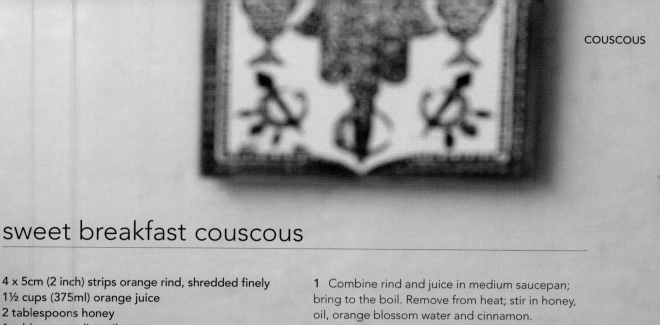

sweet breakfast couscous

4 x 5cm (2 inch) strips orange rind, shredded finely
1½ cups (375ml) orange juice
2 tablespoons honey
1 tablespoon olive oil
1 teaspoon orange blossom water
½ teaspoon ground cinnamon
1½ cups (300g) couscous
8 fresh dates (160g), seeded, quartered lengthways
⅓ cup (55g) coarsely chopped blanched
  almonds, roasted
⅓ cup (45g) coarsely chopped unsalted
  pistachios, roasted
¼ cup (40g) finely chopped dried apricots
1 cup (280g) greek-style yogurt

1 Combine rind and juice in medium saucepan; bring to the boil. Remove from heat; stir in honey, oil, orange blossom water and cinnamon.
2 Combine couscous with orange mixture in large heatproof bowl, cover; stand about 5 minutes or until liquid is absorbed, fluffing with fork occasionally.
3 Stir dates, nuts and apricots into couscous; serve with yogurt. Drizzle with a little extra honey.

prep + cook time 20 minutes **serves** 6
nutritional count per serving 15.6g total fat
(3.4g saturated fat); 1927kJ (461 cal);
65.4g carbohydrate; 13.1g protein; 3.5g fibre

roasted vegetable couscous

1 medium red onion (170g), cut into wedges
4 small zucchini (360g), halved lengthways
10 baby carrots (175g), halved lengthways
2 tablespoons olive oil
1 cup (200g) couscous
1 cup (250ml) boiling water
450g (14 ounces) bottled roasted red capsicum, drained, sliced thinly
2 tablespoons finely chopped fresh thyme

1 Preheat oven to 220°C/425°F.
2 Combine onion, zucchini, carrot and oil in large shallow baking dish; season. Roast, uncovered, about 20 minutes or until vegetables are tender.
3 Combine couscous with the water in large heatproof bowl, cover; stand about 5 minutes or until liquid is absorbed, fluffing with fork occasionally.
4 Stir vegetables and remaining ingredients into couscous; season to taste.

prep + cook time 35 minutes **serves** 6
nutritional count per serving 8.3g total fat (1.3g saturated fat); 995kJ (238 cal); 32.1g carbohydrate; 6.7g protein; 3.3g fibre

Serve with a dollop of sheep's-milk yogurt.

note To save time, use any leftover or store-bought roasted vegetables in this recipe.

preserved lemon and olive couscous

1¼ cups (250g) couscous
1¼ cups (310ml) boiling water
15g (½ ounce) butter
400g (15 ounces) canned chickpeas
  (garbanzo beans), rinsed, drained
½ cup (60g) seeded green olives, chopped coarsely
2 tablespoons lemon juice
3 green onions (scallions), sliced thinly
2 tablespoons finely chopped fresh flat-leaf parsley
1 tablespoon thinly sliced preserved lemon rind

1 Combine couscous with the water and butter in large heatproof bowl, cover; stand about 5 minutes or until water is absorbed, fluffing with fork occasionally.
2 Stir remaining ingredients into couscous; season to taste.

prep time 15 minutes **serves** 6
nutritional count per serving 5.3g total fat (1.8g saturated fat); 1020kJ (244 cal); 38.5g carbohydrate; 8.5g protein; 3g fibre

spiced cauliflower couscous

1 tablespoon olive oil
1 small brown onion (80g), sliced thinly
1 teaspoon ground coriander
½ small cauliflower (500g), cut into small florets
2 tablespoons water
⅓ cup coarsely chopped fresh coriander (cilantro)
1¼ cups (250g) couscous
1¼ cups (310ml) boiling water

1   Heat oil in large saucepan, add onion; cook, stirring, until onion is soft. Add ground coriander and cauliflower; cook, stirring, until fragrant. Add the water; cook, covered, about 10 minutes or until cauliflower is tender and water absorbed. Stir in half the fresh coriander.
2   Meanwhile, combine couscous with the boiling water in large heatproof bowl, cover; stand about 5 minutes or until liquid is absorbed, fluffing with fork occasionally.
3   Stir cauliflower mixture into couscous; season to taste. Serve sprinkled with remaining fresh coriander.

prep + cook time 25 minutes **serves** 6
nutritional count per serving 3.4g total fat
(0.5g saturated fat); 844kJ (202 cal);
34.2g carbohydrate; 7.1g protein; 1.9g fibre

baked tomato couscous

1 cup (250ml) chicken stock
1 cup (200g) couscous
15g (½ ounce) butter
2 trimmed medium silver beet leaves (160g),
  shredded finely
410g (13 ounces) canned tomato puree
½ cup (60g) coarsely grated gruyère cheese

1   Preheat oven to 200°C/400°F. Oil shallow
1-litre (4-cup) ovenproof dish.
2   Bring stock to the boil in medium saucepan;
remove from heat, add couscous and butter. Cover;
stand about 5 minutes or until liquid is absorbed,
fluffing with fork occasionally. Stir silver beet into
couscous; season to taste.
3   Spoon couscous into dish; press down gently.
Pour tomato over couscous, sprinkle with cheese.
4   Bake about 30 minutes or until cheese is
browned lightly.

prep + cook time 45 minutes **serves** 6
nutritional count per serving 5.9g total fat
(3.6g saturated fat); 882kJ (211 cal);
29.6g carbohydrate; 8.5g protein; 1.9g fibre

note To make this a vegetarian couscous, replace
the chicken stock with vegetable stock.

spicy red couscous

1 tablespoon olive oil
1 tablespoon harissa paste
2 teaspoons sweet paprika
4 green onions (scallions), sliced thinly
1 cup (250ml) chicken stock
½ cup (125ml) water
1½ cups (300g) couscous
1 tablespoon lemon juice

1   Heat oil in medium saucepan, add harissa, paprika and half the onion; cook, stirring, about 2 minutes or until fragrant. Add stock and the water; bring to the boil. Remove from heat, add couscous; cover, stand about 5 minutes or until liquid is absorbed, fluffing with fork occasionally.
2   Stir juice into couscous; season to taste. Serve sprinkled with remaining onion.

prep + cook time 15 minutes **serves** 6
nutritional count per serving 3.6g total fat
(0.6g saturated fat); 928kJ (222 cal);
39.4g carbohydrate; 7g protein; 0.7g fibre

pumpkin, apricot and cheese couscous

750g (1½ pounds) pumpkin, unpeeled,
  cut into wedges
2 tablespoons olive oil
1 cup (200g) couscous
2 tablespoons finely grated lemon rind
1 cup (250ml) boiling water
1 cup (150g) dried apricots, halved
½ cup (80g) pepitas
2 tablespoons lemon juice
2 tablespoons finely chopped fresh flat-leaf parsley
125g (4 ounces) soft goat's cheese, crumbled

1 Preheat oven to 200°C/400°F.
2 Combine pumpkin and oil in medium shallow baking dish. Roast, uncovered, about 20 minutes or until pumpkin is tender.
3 Meanwhile, combine couscous, rind and the water in large heatproof bowl, cover; stand about 5 minutes or until liquid is absorbed, fluffing with fork occasionally.
4 Stir apricots, pepitas, juice and parsley into couscous; season to taste.
5 Top couscous with pumpkin; sprinkle over cheese.

prep + cook time 30 minutes **serves** 6
nutritional count per serving 16.1g total fat (4.3g saturated fat); 1643kJ (393 cal); 45.5g carbohydrate; 13.6g protein; 5.4g fibre

tagines

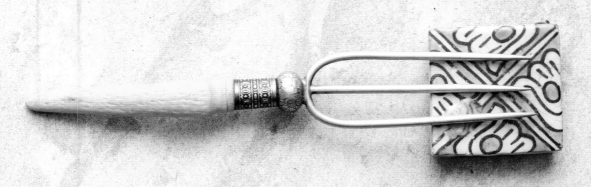

chicken tagine with olives and lemon

2kg (4 pound) whole chicken
2 teaspoons each ground ginger, cumin
  and coriander
1 tablespoon olive oil
1 large brown onion (200g), sliced thickly
3 cloves garlic, crushed
¼ teaspoon ground turmeric
pinch saffron threads
1 cup (250ml) water
1 cup (250ml) chicken stock
625g (1¼ pounds) baby new potatoes, halved
375g (12 ounces) jap pumpkin, unpeeled, cut
  into wedges
1 cup (120g) seeded green olives
2 tablespoons thinly sliced preserved lemon rind
2 tablespoons lemon juice
½ cup coarsely chopped fresh flat-leaf parsley
¼ cup coarsely chopped fresh coriander (cilantro)

1 Rinse chicken under cold water; pat dry inside and out with absorbent paper. Using kitchen scissors, cut along both sides of backbone; discard backbone. Press down on breastbone to flatten out chicken. Combine half the combined ginger, cumin and coriander in small bowl; rub mixture over chicken.
2 Preheat oven to 220°C/425°F.
3 Heat oil in tagine or flameproof casserole dish on stove top; cook chicken until browned all over. Remove from tagine. Reserve 1 tablespoon pan drippings; discard remainder.
4 Heat reserved pan drippings in same tagine; stir onion and garlic until soft. Add turmeric and saffron, and remaining ginger, cumin and coriander; cook, stirring, about 1 minute or until fragrant. Add the water, stock, potatoes and pumpkin; top with chicken. Bring to the boil.
5 Cover tagine, transfer to oven; cook about 1¼ hours or until chicken is cooked.
6 Stir olives, preserved lemon and juice into sauce; season to taste. Serve tagine sprinkled with herbs.

prep + cook time 2 hours serves 6
nutritional count per serving 34.5g total fat
(9.6g saturated fat); 2316kJ (554 cal);
20.1g carbohydrate; 38.4g protein; 4.4g fibre

Serve with couscous.

lamb tfaya

1kg (2 pounds) boned lamb shoulder,
  chopped coarsely
1 tablespoon ground ginger
2 teaspoons ras el hanout
1 teaspoon ground cinnamon
2 tablespoons olive oil
1 litre (4 cups) water
2 cups (500ml) chicken stock
400g (15 ounces) canned chickpeas
  (garbanzo beans), rinsed, drained
2 cups (400g) couscous
2 cups (500ml) boiling water
15g (½ ounce) butter
¼ cup finely chopped fresh coriander (cilantro)
½ cup (80g) coarsely chopped blanched
  almonds, roasted
3 hard-boiled eggs, quartered
TFAYA
2 large brown onions (400g), sliced thinly
¼ cup (90g) honey
½ cup (75g) raisins
45g (1½ ounces) butter, chopped
1 teaspoon each ground white pepper
  and cinnamon
½ teaspoon ground turmeric
pinch saffron threads
½ cup (125ml) water

1 Combine lamb and spices in large bowl. Heat oil in large saucepan; cook lamb, in batches, until browned all over.
2 Return lamb to pan with the water, stock and chickpeas; bring to the boil. Reduce heat; simmer, covered, 30 minutes. Uncover; simmer, stirring occasionally, about 1 hour or until lamb is tender.
3 Meanwhile, make tfaya.
4 Combine couscous with the boiling water and butter in large heatproof bowl, cover; stand about 5 minutes or until liquid is absorbed, fluffing with fork occasionally.
5 Stir coriander and nuts into couscous; season to taste. Serve lamb mixture with couscous; accompany with tfaya and eggs.
TFAYA Combine ingredients in medium saucepan; bring to the boil. Reduce heat; simmer, uncovered, stirring occasionally, about 30 minutes or until onion is caramelised.

prep + cook time 1 hour 50 minutes serves 6
nutritional count per serving 36.2g total fat (12.6g saturated fat); 3674kJ (879 cal); 83.2g carbohydrate; 53.5g protein; 5.3g fibre

note Tfaya is an accompaniment of sweet and spicy caramelised onions and raisins.

chilli fish tagine

4 x 200g (6½ ounces) white fish fillets, skin on
1 tablespoon finely grated lemon rind
2 teaspoons dried chilli flakes
2 cloves garlic, crushed
1 tablespoon mustard seed oil
30g (1 ounce) butter
2 baby fennel bulbs (260g), trimmed,
  cut into wedges
150g (5 ounces) green beans, halved lengthways
⅓ cup (50g) raisins
1 cup (250ml) dry white wine
pinch saffron threads
⅓ cup (45g) roasted unsalted pistachios

1 Combine fish, rind, chilli, garlic and oil in large mixing bowl; cover, refrigerate 3 hours or overnight.
2 Melt butter in tagine or large frying pan; cook fennel, stirring, until browned lightly. Add beans, raisins, wine and saffron; top with fish. Bring to the boil. Reduce heat; simmer, covered, about 15 minutes or until fish is cooked as desired. Season to taste.
3 Serve tagine sprinkled with nuts.

prep + cook time 30 minutes (+ refrigeration)
serves 4
nutritional count per serving 21.1g total fat (6.7g saturated fat); 1956kJ (468 cal); 13.1g carbohydrate; 44.8g protein; 4g fibre

notes We used blue-eye fillets in this recipe but you can use any firm white fish fillets.
Fish or chicken stock can be used instead of wine.
Mustard seed oil has a lovely flavour; it can be found in health-food shops, delis and some supermarkets. If you like, use olive oil instead.

tuna tagine with lentils and beans

4 x 185g (6 ounces) tuna steaks (see notes)
2 teaspoons each ground cumin and coriander
½ teaspoon dried chilli flakes
¼ cup (60ml) olive oil
⅓ cup finely chopped fresh flat-leaf parsley
2 large carrots (360g), cut into matchsticks
2 cups (500ml) chicken consommé (see notes)
1 tablespoon honey
800g (31 ounces) canned brown lentils,
  rinsed, drained
¾ cup frozen broad beans (90g), thawed, peeled
1 tablespoon coarsely chopped fresh
  flat-leaf parsley, extra

1 Combine tuna, spices, chilli, half the oil and
half the parsley in large bowl. Cover, refrigerate
3 hours or overnight.
2 Heat remaining oil in tagine or large frying pan;
cook carrots, stirring, until tender. Add consommé,
honey, lentils and half the beans; top with tuna.
Bring to the boil, reduce heat; simmer, covered,
about 10 minutes or until tuna is cooked as desired.
Season to taste.
3 Stir in remaining beans; stand tagine, covered,
5 minutes; serve sprinkled with extra parsley.

prep + cook time 30 minutes (+ refrigeration)
serves 4
nutritional count per serving 25.3g total fat
(6.4g saturated fat); 2299kJ (550 cal);
21g carbohydrate; 56.2g protein; 7.2g fibre

notes Ask your fishmonger to cut thick tuna steaks;
thin steaks can easily overcook and dry out.
Use either canned or packaged consommé for a
good flavour, but if you prefer, use stock instead.

chicken tagine with prunes

2kg (4 pound) whole chicken (see notes)
2 tablespoons moroccan seasoning
¼ cup (35g) plain (all-purpose) flour
1 tablespoon olive oil
8 shallots (200g)
1 cup (170g) seeded prunes, halved
¾ cup (120g) blanched almonds, roasted
4 trimmed silver beet (swiss chard) leaves (320g), shredded finely
2 cups (500ml) chicken consommé (see notes)
½ cup (125ml) prune juice
2 tablespoons finely chopped fresh flat-leaf parsley

1 Preheat oven to 200°C/400°F.
2 Rinse chicken under cold water; pat dry inside and out with absorbent paper. Using kitchen scissors, cut chicken into four pieces.
3 Combine seasoning and flour in large bowl; coat chicken with flour mixture, shake off excess.
4 Heat oil in tagine or flameproof casserole dish on stove top; cook chicken, in batches, until browned. Remove from tagine; drain on absorbent paper.
5 Meanwhile, peel shallots, leaving root ends intact. Cook shallots in same heated tagine, stirring, until browned. Add prunes, nuts, half the silver beet, consommé, juice and parsley; bring to the boil. Top with chicken.
6 Cover tagine, transfer to oven; cook about 50 minutes or until chicken is cooked. Remove from oven; stir in remaining silver beet. Season to taste. Stand tagine, covered, 10 minutes before serving.

prep + cook time 1 hour 5 minutes serves 4
nutritional count per serving 62.4g total fat (14.4g saturated fat); 3954kJ (946 cal); 33.5g carbohydrate; 61g protein; 7.9g fibre

notes Ask the butcher to cut the chicken into four pieces for you, or buy four chicken marylands. Use either canned or packaged consommé for a good flavour, but if you prefer, use stock instead.

lamb tagine with ras el hanout

750g (1½ pounds) boned lamb shoulder,
  chopped coarsely
2 tablespoons ras el hanout
¼ cup (60ml) olive oil
8 baby new potatoes (320g), halved
2 small leeks (400g), sliced thinly
4 cups (1 litre) beef consommé (see note)
2 tablespoons finely chopped fresh flat-leaf parsley

1 Combine lamb, ras el hanout and 1 tablespoon of the oil in large bowl. Cover, refrigerate 3 hours or overnight.
2 Preheat oven to 200°C/400°F.
3 Heat 1 tablespoon of the remaining oil in tagine or flameproof casserole dish on stove top; cook lamb, in batches, until browned. Remove from tagine.
4 Heat remaining oil in same tagine; cook potato and leek, stirring, until potatoes are browned lightly and leek softens. Return lamb to tagine with consommé; bring to the boil.
5 Cover tagine, transfer to oven; cook about 45 minutes or until lamb is tender. Remove from oven; stir in parsley. Season to taste.

prep + cook time 1 hour (+ refrigeration) **serves** 4
nutritional count per serving 25.7g total fat
(7.5g saturated fat); 2023kJ (484 cal);
16.9g carbohydrate; 44.2g protein; 4.7g fibre

note Use either canned or packaged consommé for a good flavour, but if you prefer, use stock instead.

meatball tagine with eggs

500g (1 pound) minced (ground) beef
1 clove garlic, crushed
¼ cup finely chopped fresh mint
2 tablespoons finely chopped fresh coriander
  (cilantro)
1 teaspoon each ground cinnamon and coriander
2 teaspoons ground cumin
½ teaspoon chilli powder
1 tablespoon olive oil
1 medium brown onion (150g), chopped finely
4 large tomatoes (880g), chopped coarsely
pinch saffron threads
4 eggs
½ cup loosely packed fresh coriander
  (cilantro) leaves

1 Combine mince, garlic, mint, chopped coriander, cinnamon, ground coriander, half the cumin and half the chilli in large bowl; season. Roll level tablespoons of mixture into balls.
2 Heat oil in tagine or large frying pan; cook meatballs, in batches, until browned. Remove from tagine.
3 Stir onion in same heated tagine until softened. Add tomato, saffron and remaining cumin and chilli; bring to the boil. Simmer, uncovered, about 15 minutes or until tomatoes soften.
4 Return meatballs to pan; simmer, uncovered, about 10 minutes or until meatballs are cooked and sauce thickens slightly. Season to taste. Carefully crack eggs into tagine; simmer, covered, about 5 minutes or until eggs are barely set. Sprinkle tagine with coriander leaves.

prep + cook time 1 hour **serves** 4
nutritional count per serving 20.2g total fat (7.1g saturated fat); 1488kJ (356 cal); 6.6g carbohydrate; 35.3g protein; 3.5g fibre

Serve with crusty bread.

lamb kefta tagine

625g (1¼ pounds) minced (ground) lamb
2 cloves garlic, crushed
1 medium red onion (170g), chopped finely
1 tablespoon each ground cumin, coriander and
  sweet paprika
1 cup firmly packed fresh coriander leaves (cilantro)
2 fresh small red thai (serrano) chillies, sliced thinly
2 eggs
1 cup (70g) stale breadcrumbs
½ cup (125ml) beef stock
800g (28 ounces) canned diced tomatoes
1 cup (150g) drained semi-dried tomatoes,
  chopped coarsely
½ cup firmly packed fresh basil leaves,
  chopped coarsely

1 Preheat oven to 200°C/400°F.
2 Combine mince, garlic, onion, spices, coriander leaves, chilli, eggs and breadcrumbs in large bowl; season. Roll 2 heaped tablespoons of mixture into balls.
3 Cook meatballs, in batches, in heated oiled tagine or flameproof casserole dish, on stove top, until browned. Remove from tagine; drain meatballs on absorbent paper.
4 Return meatballs to tagine with stock, undrained tomatoes, semi-dried tomatoes and basil; bring to the boil.
5 Cover tagine, transfer to oven; cook about 35 minutes or until meatballs are cooked through. Season to taste.

prep + cook time 55 minutes **serves** 4
nutritional count per serving 17.5g total fat
(6.6g saturated fat); 2086kJ (499 cal);
34.5g carbohydrate; 45.2g protein; 9.7g fibre

Serve with rice and flat bread.

beef and eggplant tagine

2 tablespoons olive oil
625g (1¼ pounds) beef chuck steak,
  chopped coarsely
1 medium brown onion (150g), chopped coarsely
2 cloves garlic, crushed
2 teaspoons ground coriander
1 teaspoon each ground ginger, cumin and
  sweet paprika
½ cup (125ml) beef stock
3 medium tomatoes (450g), chopped coarsely
3 baby eggplants (180g), sliced thickly

1 Heat half the oil in tagine or large saucepan; cook
beef, in batches, until browned. Remove from tagine.
2 Stir onion in same heated tagine until softened.
Add garlic and spices; cook, stirring, until fragrant.
Return beef to tagine with stock and tomato;
bring to the boil. Reduce heat; simmer, covered,
45 minutes. Uncover; simmer about 30 minutes or
until beef is tender and tagine thickens.
3 Meanwhile, heat remaining oil in medium frying
pan; cook eggplant, stirring, about 10 minutes or
until browned and tender. Stir eggplant into tagine;
season to taste.

prep + cook time 1 hour 30 minutes serves 4
nutritional count per serving 21.2g total fat
(5.9g saturated fat); 1538kJ (368 cal);
5.7g carbohydrate; 37.3g protein; 3.1g fibre

beef, raisin and almond tagine

1 tablespoon olive oil
625g (1¼ pounds) beef chuck steak,
  chopped coarsely
1 medium brown onion (150g), chopped coarsely
2 cloves garlic, crushed
2 teaspoons ras el hanout
½ teaspoon each ground ginger and cinnamon
1 dried bay leaf
1 cup (250ml) beef stock
¼ cup (35g) coarsely chopped raisins
¼ cup (40g) blanched almonds, roasted

1   Heat oil in tagine or large frying pan; cook beef, in batches, until browned. Remove from tagine.
2   Stir onion in same heated tagine until softened. Add garlic, spices and bay leaf; cook, stirring, until fragrant. Return beef to pan with stock; bring to the boil. Reduce heat; simmer, covered, 1 hour. Add raisins; simmer, uncovered, about 15 minutes or until beef is tender and tagine thickens. Stir in nuts, season to taste; accompany with lemon wedges.

prep + cook time 1 hour 30 minutes serves 4
nutritional count per serving 22.1g total fat
(5.6g saturated fat); 1630kJ (390 cal);
9.2g carbohydrate; 38.3g protein; 2.1g fibre

lamb, artichoke and capsicum tagine

1kg (2 pounds) boned lamb shoulder,
  chopped coarsely
2 teaspoons each ground ginger and cinnamon
1 teaspoon hot paprika
2 tablespoons olive oil
1 large red onion (300g), sliced thickly
3 cloves garlic, crushed
1½ cups (375ml) beef stock
340g (11 ounces) bottled marinated artichoke
  hearts, drained, halved
½ cup (80g) drained, thinly sliced bottled roasted
  red capsicum (bell pepper)
¼ cup (40g) thinly sliced preserved lemon rind
¼ cup coarsely chopped fresh flat-leaf parsley

1 Combine lamb and half the combined spices in large bowl.
2 Heat half the oil in tagine or flameproof casserole dish; cook lamb, in batches, until browned. Remove from tagine.
3 Heat remaining oil in same tagine, add onion and garlic; cook, stirring, until soft. Add remaining spices; cook, stirring, about 1 minute or until fragrant. Return lamb to tagine with stock; bring to the boil. Reduce heat; simmer, covered, about 50 minutes or until lamb is tender.
4 Add artichokes, capsicum and rind; simmer, uncovered, until heated through. Season to taste.
5 Serve tagine sprinkled with parsley.

prep + cook time 1 hour 30 minutes **serves** 6
nutritional count per serving 16.3g total fat
(5.5g saturated fat); 1321kJ (316 cal);
4.6g carbohydrate; 36g protein; 2.7g fibre

Serve with couscous.

white bean and lentil tagine

1 tablespoon olive oil

1 medium brown onion (150g), chopped coarsely

2 cloves garlic, crushed

2.5cm (1 inch) piece fresh ginger (15g),
  cut into matchsticks

1 teaspoon harissa paste

800g (28 ounces) canned whole peeled tomatoes,
  chopped coarsely

1 medium red capsicum (bell pepper) (200g),
  chopped coarsely

½ cup (125ml) water

400g (14 ounces) canned cannellini beans,
  rinsed, drained

400g (14 ounces) canned brown lentils,
  rinsed, drained

¼ cup finely chopped fresh mint

¼ cup finely chopped fresh flat-leaf parsley

1 Heat oil in tagine or large frying pan; stir onion until softened. Add garlic, ginger and paste; cook, stirring, about 1 minute or until fragrant.

2 Add undrained tomatoes, capsicum, the water, beans and lentils; bring to the boil. Reduce heat; simmer, uncovered, about 15 minutes or until tagine thickens. Remove from heat; stir in mint, season to taste.

3 Serve tagine sprinkled with parsley.

prep + cook time 40 minutes **serves** 4
nutritional count per serving 5.8g total fat
(0.8g saturated fat); 865kJ (207 cal);
23.8g carbohydrate; 10.6g protein; 10.2g fibre

Serve with grilled flatbread.

lamb and quince tagine

45g (1½ ounces) butter
2 tablespoons olive oil
2 medium quinces (700g), peeled, cut into
  thick wedges
¼ cup (90g) honey
1kg (2 pounds) boned lamb shoulder,
  chopped coarsely
2 tablespoons finely chopped fresh coriander
  (cilantro) root and stem mixture
2 teaspoons each ground cumin and coriander
1 teaspoon ground ginger
1 cinnamon stick
1½ cups (375ml) beef stock
2 tablespoons tomato paste
¼ cup (40g) dried currants
½ cup loosely packed fresh coriander
  (cilantro) leaves

1 Heat butter and half the oil in tagine or
flameproof casserole dish; cook quince, stirring,
about 10 minutes or until browned lightly. Add
half the honey; cook, stirring, about 5 minutes or
until quince is lightly caramelised. Remove quince
from tagine.
2 Preheat oven to 180°C/350°F.
3 Heat remaining oil in same tagine; cook lamb,
in batches, until browned.
4 Return lamb and quince to tagine with coriander
root and stem mixture, spices, stock, paste and
remaining honey; bring to the boil.
5 Cover tagine, transfer to oven; cook about
1½ hours or until lamb is tender.
6 Remove from oven; stir in currants and coriander
leaves. Season to taste.

prep + cook time 2 hours **serves** 6
nutritional count per serving 22.1g total fat
(9.5g saturated fat); 1902kJ (455 cal);
26.7g carbohydrate; 35g protein; 6.7g fibre

note Some of the stems and roots of coriander are
used in this recipe so buy a bunch of fresh coriander
with its roots intact. Wash the coriander under cold
water, removing any dirt clinging to the roots. Chop
coriander roots and stems together to obtain the
amount specified.

chicken tagine with figs and walnuts

½ cup (55g) coarsely chopped roasted walnuts
4 chicken drumsticks (600g)
4 chicken thigh cutlets (800g)
2 teaspoons cumin seeds
2 teaspoons each ground ginger and cinnamon
1 tablespoon olive oil
1 large red onion (300g), sliced thickly
pinch saffron threads
1½ cups (375ml) chicken stock
1 tablespoon honey
6 medium fresh figs (360g), halved
1 teaspoon white sugar
45g (1½ ounces) baby spinach leaves
¼ cup finely chopped fresh flat-leaf parsley

1 Dry-fry nuts in tagine or flameproof casserole dish until browned lightly. Remove from tagine.
2 Combine chicken and cumin seeds with half the ginger and half the cinnamon in large bowl.
3 Heat oil in same tagine; cook chicken, in batches, until browned. Remove from tagine. Reserve 1 tablespoon pan drippings; discard remainder.
4 Heat reserved pan drippings in same tagine; stir onion until soft. Add saffron and remaining ginger and cinnamon; cook, stirring, about 2 minutes or until fragrant. Return chicken to tagine with stock; bring to the boil. Reduce heat; simmer, covered, about 30 minutes or until chicken is cooked.
5 Remove chicken from tagine; cover to keep warm. Add honey to tagine; simmer, uncovered, about 10 minutes or until sauce is browned and thickened slightly.
6 Meanwhile, place figs, cut-side up, on a baking (parchment) paper lined oven tray; sprinkle with sugar. Cook under preheated grill (broiler) about 5 minutes or until browned lightly.
7 Return chicken to tagine with spinach; simmer, covered, until heated through. Season to taste.
8 Serve tagine topped with figs; sprinkle with nuts and parsley.

prep + cook time 1 hour 10 minutes **serves** 6
nutritional count per serving 30.2g total fat (7.5g saturated fat); 1873kJ (448 cal); 12.9g carbohydrate; 30.5g protein; 3.1g fibre

Serve with couscous.

chermoulla fish tagine

4 x 200g (6½ ounces) white fish fillets, skin on
¼ cup (60ml) olive oil
500g (1 pound) small red-skinned potatoes,
  unpeeled, sliced thickly
500g (1 pound) cherry truss tomatoes
½ cup (125ml) chicken stock
2 tablespoons tomato paste
1 teaspoon white sugar
¼ cup each loosely packed fresh flat-leaf parsley
  leaves and mint leaves
CHERMOULLA
¼ cup each coarsely chopped fresh flat-leaf
  parsley and coriander (cilantro)
2 tablespoons lemon juice
1 tablespoon olive oil
2 cloves garlic, halved
2 teaspoons each ground cumin and sweet paprika
2 teaspoons harissa paste

1 Make chermoulla.
2 Combine fish and chermoulla in large bowl.
Cover, refrigerate 30 minutes.
3 Heat half the oil in tagine or flameproof casserole
dish, add potato; cook, stirring, about 10 minutes
or until browned lightly. Cover; cook 5 minutes or
until potatoes are almost tender.
4 Uncover potatoes; top with fish and tomatoes.
Combine stock, tomato paste and sugar in medium
jug; season. Pour stock mixture over fish in tagine;
bring to the boil. Reduce heat; simmer, covered,
about 20 minutes or until fish is cooked.
5 Serve tagine drizzled with remaining oil; sprinkle
with herbs.
CHERMOULLA Blend or process ingredients until
almost smooth.

prep + cook time 50 minutes (+ refrigeration)
serves 4
nutritional count per serving 23.2g total fat
(4.1g saturated fat); 2077kJ (497 cal);
22.8g carbohydrate; 45.6g protein; 5.9g fibre

notes We used snapper fillets for this recipe but
you can use any white fish fillets.
We used desiree potatoes in this recipe.

sweet and spicy vegetable tagine

2 tablespoons olive oil
1 medium brown onion (150g), sliced thinly
5cm (2 inch) piece fresh ginger (25g), grated
2 cloves garlic, crushed
2 teaspoons each ground cumin and coriander
1 teaspoon sweet paprika
500g (1 pound) pumpkin, chopped coarsely
1 medium kumara (orange sweet potato) (400g),
  chopped coarsely
2 small parsnips (240g), chopped coarsely
2 cups (500ml) vegetable stock
400g (14 ounces) canned diced tomatoes
2 tablespoons honey
8 small yellow patty pan squash (185g), halved
375g (12 ounces) baby carrots, trimmed
⅓ cup (50g) raisins
2 tablespoons finely chopped fresh flat-leaf parsley
¼ cup (20g) flaked almonds, roasted

1   Heat oil in tagine or flameproof casserole dish,
add onion; cook, stirring, until softened. Add
ginger, garlic and spices; cook, stirring, about
1 minute or until fragrant.
2   Add pumpkin, kumara, parsnip, stock, undrained
tomatoes and honey; bring to the boil. Reduce
heat; simmer, covered, 15 minutes. Add squash
and carrots; simmer, uncovered, 20 minutes or until
vegetables are tender. Season to taste.
3   Stir in raisins and parsley; sprinkle with nuts.

prep + cook time 55 minutes **serves** 8
nutritional count per serving 6.8g total fat
(1g saturated fat); 857kJ (205 cal);
28.4g carbohydrate; 5.4g protein; 5.3g fibre

veal, quince and caramelised onion tagine

6 baby brown onions (150g)
6 thick pieces veal knuckle (1.6kg)
2 teaspoons each ground ginger and cinnamon
½ teaspoon chilli powder
1 tablespoon olive oil
1 tablespoon honey
2½ cups (625ml) beef stock
3 cloves garlic, crushed
3 medium quinces (1kg), peeled, cored,
  cut into thick wedges
⅓ cup coarsely chopped fresh coriander (cilantro)

1 Peel onions, leaving root ends intact; halve onions.
2 Combine veal and half the combined spices in large bowl.
3 Heat half the oil in tagine or flameproof casserole dish; cook veal, in batches, until browned. Remove from tagine.
4 Heat remaining oil in same tagine; cook onion, honey and ½ cup of the stock, stirring occasionally, about 5 minutes or until onion caramelises. Remove from tagine.
5 Add garlic and remaining spices to tagine; cook, stirring, about 1 minute or until fragrant. Return veal to tagine with remaining stock and quince; bring to the boil. Reduce heat; simmer, covered, about 1½ hours or until veal is tender.
6 Add onion to tagine; simmer, covered, about 5 minutes or until heated through. Season to taste.
7 Serve tagine sprinkled with coriander.

prep + cook time 2 hours 15 minutes **serves** 6
nutritional count per serving 19.2g total fat (7.7g saturated fat); 1739kJ (416 cal); 18.7g carbohydrate; 38g protein; 9.2g fibre

Serve with couscous.

note Ask your butcher to cut the veal knuckle into 6 thick slices for you. You could use veal osso buco if you can't get veal knuckle.

lamb tagine with sweet prunes

1kg (2 pounds) boned lamb shoulder,
  chopped coarsely
⅓ cup (80ml) olive oil
2 medium red onions (340g), grated coarsely
4 cloves garlic, crushed
1 teaspoon each ground ginger and sweet paprika
¼ teaspoon each dried chilli flakes and
  saffron threads
800g (28 ounces) canned diced tomatoes
4 x 5cm (2 inch) strips orange rind
2 cinnamon sticks
½ cup coarsely chopped fresh coriander (cilantro)
SWEET PRUNES
18 seeded prunes (145g)
¼ cup (90g) honey
2 tablespoons water

1 Combine lamb, oil, onion, garlic and spices in large bowl. Cover, refrigerate 3 hours or overnight.
2 Preheat oven to 180°C/350°F.
3 Heat oiled tagine or flameproof casserole dish on stove top; cook lamb, in batches, until browned.
4 Return lamb to tagine with undrained tomatoes, rind, cinnamon sticks and half the coriander; bring to the boil.
5 Cover tagine, transfer to oven; cook about 1½ hours or until lamb is tender.
6 Meanwhile, make sweet prunes.
7 Serve tagine with sweet prunes; sprinkle with remaining coriander.
SWEET PRUNES Combine ingredients in small saucepan; bring to the boil. Reduce heat; simmer, uncovered, 10 minutes.

prep + cook time 1 hour 50 minutes (+ refrigeration)
serves 6
nutritional count per serving 22.1g total fat (6.2g saturated fat); 1969kJ (471 cal); 30.5g carbohydrate; 35.9g protein; 4.6g fibre

spicy prawn and tomato tagine

1 tablespoon olive oil
1 medium brown onion (150g), chopped finely
3 cloves garlic, crushed
1 teaspoon each ground ginger and cumin
¼ teaspoon chilli powder
pinch saffron threads
1kg (2 pounds) tomatoes, chopped coarsely
1.5kg (3¼ pounds) uncooked medium king prawns
¼ cup each finely chopped fresh flat-leaf parsley
  and coriander (cilantro)
¼ cup (30g) finely chopped roasted
  unsalted pistachios
1 tablespoon finely chopped preserved lemon rind

1 Heat oil in tagine or flameproof casserole dish; cook onion and garlic, stirring, until onion softens. Add spices; cook, stirring, about 1 minute or until fragrant. Add tomato; cook, stirring, about 5 minutes or until tomato softens. Bring to the boil. Reduce heat; simmer, stirring occasionally, about 10 minutes or until sauce thickens slightly.
2 Meanwhile, shell and devein prawns leaving tails intact. Add prawns to pan; cook, covered, stirring occasionally, about 5 minutes or until prawns are changed in colour. Season to taste.
3 Combine herbs, nuts and preserved lemon in small bowl.
4 Serve tagine sprinkled with herb mixture.

prep + cook time 40 minutes **serves** 6
nutritional count per serving 6.6g total fat
(0.9g saturated fat); 857kJ (205 cal);
5.5g carbohydrate; 28.8g protein; 3.2g fibre

Serve with couscous or crusty bread.

roasts & kebabs

roast chicken with couscous stuffing

½ cup (100g) couscous
½ cup (125ml) boiling water
2 tablespoons honey
½ teaspoon each ground cumin and coriander
¼ teaspoon ground cinnamon
2 tablespoons coarsely chopped raisins
2 tablespoons coarsely chopped dried apricots
1.6kg (3¼ pound) whole chicken
⅓ cup (80ml) orange juice
1 teaspoon dried oregano
½ teaspoon sweet paprika
1 cup (250ml) water
ORANGE HONEY YOGURT
¾ cup (200g) yogurt
2 teaspoons honey
1 teaspoon finely grated orange rind

1 Combine couscous with the boiling water and honey in small heatproof bowl, cover; stand about 5 minutes or until liquid is absorbed, fluffing with fork occasionally. Stir in cumin, coriander, cinnamon and fruit. Season to taste.
2 Preheat oven to 200°C/400°F.
3 Rinse chicken under cold water; pat dry inside and out with absorbent paper. Tuck wing tips under chicken. Trim skin around neck; secure neck flap to underside of chicken with skewers. Fill cavity with couscous mixture, fold skin to enclose stuffing; secure with skewers. Tie legs together with kitchen string.
4 Place chicken in oiled medium baking dish. Drizzle chicken with juice, sprinkle with oregano and paprika; pour the water into dish. Season. Roast chicken about 1½ hours, basting occasionally with juices, or until chicken is cooked.
5 Meanwhile, make orange honey yogurt.
6 Serve chicken with stuffing and yogurt.
ORANGE HONEY YOGURT Combine ingredients in small bowl.

prep + cook time 1 hour 50 minutes **serves** 4
nutritional count per serving 33.5g total fat (10.8g saturated fat); 2776kJ (664 cal); 44.3g carbohydrate; 46g protein; 2.1g fibre

vegetable brochettes

2 cloves garlic, crushed
¼ cup (30g) dukkah
1 tablespoon finely grated lemon rind
½ cup (125ml) olive oil
12 shallots (300g), peeled
250g (8 ounces) cherry truss tomatoes
2 medium zucchini (240g), cut into six pieces each
12 baby beetroot (300g), trimmed
36 fresh bay leaves

1 To make dressing, combine garlic, dukkah, rind and oil in screw-top jar; shake well.
2 Combine shallots, tomatoes, zucchini and half the dressing in large bowl.
3 Place beetroot in medium saucepan, cover with cold water; bring to the boil. Boil for 15 minutes; drain, cool. Using disposable gloves, squeeze skins from each beetroot.
4 Thread shallots, tomatoes, zucchini, beetroot and bay leaves onto 12 metal skewers.
5 Cook brochettes on heated oiled grill plate (or grill or barbecue) about 15 minutes or until vegetables are tender. Season to taste.
6 Serve brochettes drizzled with remaining dressing.

prep + cook time 40 minutes **makes** 12
nutritional count per brochette 10.6g total fat
(1.5g saturated fat); 493kJ (118 cal);
3.7g carbohydrate; 1.5g protein; 1.9g fibre

Serve with yogurt.

notes Cut vegetables the same size for even cooking. If you have time, the shallot mixture will develop more flavour if it's covered and refrigerated overnight.

roasted harissa chicken

1.8kg (3¾ pound) whole chicken
¾ cup (225g) harissa sauce
1 large carrot (180g), halved lengthways
1 large red onion (300g), quartered
2 stalks celery (300g), trimmed
10 sprigs (20g) fresh lemon thyme
1 medium garlic bulb (70g), halved crossways
2 tablespoons olive oil

1 Rinse chicken under cold water; pat dry inside and out with absorbent paper. Tuck wing tips under chicken. Brush harissa all over chicken; tie legs together with kitchen string. Cover; refrigerate 3 hours or overnight.
2 Preheat oven to 200°C/400°F.
3 Combine remaining ingredients in large shallow baking dish; top with chicken; season.
4 Roast chicken about 1¼ hours or until chicken is cooked through. Cover; stand 10 minutes before serving.

prep + cook time 1 hour 35 minutes (+ refrigeration)
serves 4
nutritional count per serving 47.4g total fat (13g saturated fat); 2968kJ (710 cal); 19.6g carbohydrate; 48.1g protein; 8.4g fibre

honeyed orange quail

4 quails (640g)
1 tablespoon finely grated orange rind
½ cup (125ml) orange juice
4cm (1½ inch) piece fresh ginger (20g), grated
pinch ground turmeric
2 tablespoons olive oil
2 tablespoons honey
1 teaspoon sweet paprika
1 medium orange (240g), cut into 12 wedges
250g (8 ounces) rocket (arugula), trimmed

1 Rinse quails under cold water; pat dry inside and out with absorbent paper. Discard necks from quails. Using kitchen scissors, cut along each side of each quail's backbone; discard backbones. Skewer each quail lengthways with two skewers.
2 Combine rind, juice, ginger, turmeric, oil, honey and paprika in small bowl.
3 Cook quail on heated oiled grill plate (or grill or barbecue), basting with orange mixture, about 15 minutes or until cooked.
4 Cook orange wedges on heated oiled grill plate for last 10 minutes of quails' cooking time.
5 Serve quail with orange wedges and rocket.

prep + cook time 40 minutes serves 4
nutritional count per serving 18.4g total fat
(3.6g saturated fat); 1300kJ (311 cal);
19.2g carbohydrate; 17.2g protein; 1.9g fibre

lemony chicken kebabs

⅓ cup (80ml) olive oil

2 tablespoons coarsely chopped preserved lemon rind

2 tablespoons lemon juice

4 cloves garlic, halved

4cm (1½ inch) piece fresh ginger (20g), grated

1 teaspoon each ground coriander and cumin

½ teaspoon ground turmeric

¼ teaspoon ground cinnamon

1 tablespoon light brown sugar

2 tablespoons fresh marjoram leaves

1kg (2 pounds) chicken thigh fillets, chopped coarsely

1½ cups (420g) greek-style yogurt

⅓ cup finely chopped fresh coriander (cilantro)

1 medium lemon (140g), cut into wedges

1 Blend or process oil, preserved lemon, juice, garlic, ginger, spices, sugar and half the marjoram until almost smooth. Reserve 1 tablespoon of paste.

2 Combine chicken with remaining paste in large bowl. Cover; refrigerate 3 hours.

3 Thread chicken onto six metal skewers. Cook skewers on heated oiled grill plate (or grill or barbecue) until cooked.

4 Meanwhile, combine yogurt, coriander and the reserved tablespoon of paste in medium bowl. Season to taste.

5 Serve chicken kebabs sprinkled with remaining marjoram. Serve with yogurt and lemon wedges.

prep + cook time 35 minutes (+ refrigeration)
serves 6
nutritional count per serving 29.1g total fat
(8.6g saturated fat); 1843kJ (441 cal);
9.1g carbohydrate; 35.1g protein; 0.8g fibre

sardines with preserved lemon salsa

2 tablespoons olive oil
1 medium brown onion (150g), chopped finely
6 drained anchovy fillets
2 cloves garlic, crushed
500g (1 pound) cherry tomatoes
800g (28 ounces) canned diced tomatoes
¾ cup (90g) seeded black olives, chopped coarsely
¼ cup coarsely chopped fresh flat-leaf
  parsley leaves
12 butterflied sardines (400g)
PRESERVED LEMON SALSA
½ cup coarsely chopped fresh flat-leaf parsley
¼ cup (50g) finely chopped preserved lemon rind
1 clove garlic, crushed
2 tablespoons olive oil

1 Preheat oven to 220°C/425°F.
2 Heat oil in medium saucepan; stir onion, anchovy
and garlic, until onion softens. Add cherry tomatoes,
undrained canned tomatoes, olives and parsley;
bring to the boil. Pour tomato mixture into medium
baking dish. Place sardines, skin-side up, over
tomato mixture. Season.
3 Transfer dish to oven; roast, uncovered, about
15 minutes or until sardines are cooked.
4 Meanwhile, make preserved lemon salsa.
5 Serve sardine mixture topped with salsa.
PRESERVED LEMON SALSA Combine ingredients
in small bowl.

prep + cook time 40 minutes serves 4
nutritional count per serving 31.3g total fat
(5.2g saturated fat); 1785kJ (427 cal);
12.5g carbohydrate; 20g protein; 7.2g fibre

note Whiting or garfish fillets could be used
instead of sardines.

75

roast trout with orange almond filling

45g (1½ ounces) butter
1 small red onion (100g), chopped finely
1 stalk celery (150g), trimmed, chopped finely
4cm (1½ inch) piece fresh ginger (20g), grated
1 cinnamon stick
½ cup (100g) white medium-grain rice
1 cup (250ml) chicken stock
¼ cup (40g) blanched almonds, roasted,
  chopped finely
2 teaspoons finely grated orange rind
3 medium red capsicums (bell peppers) (600g)
4 whole rainbow trout (1.2kg)
1 medium orange (240g), peeled, sliced crossways
  into thin rounds
90g (3 ounces) baby spinach
⅓ cup loosely packed fresh mint leaves

1 Melt butter in medium saucepan; stir onion, celery, ginger and cinnamon about 5 minutes or until vegetables soften. Add rice; cook, stirring, 1 minute. Add stock; bring to the boil. Reduce heat; simmer, covered tightly, over low heat about 12 minutes or until water is absorbed. Remove from heat; stand rice, covered, 10 minutes, cool. Discard cinnamon stick; stir in nuts and rind.
2 Meanwhile, preheat oven to 200°C/400°F.
3 Quarter capsicums through stems, leaving stem quarters attached to capsicums; discard seeds and membranes. Divide capsicum quarters between two oiled baking dishes.
4 Fill fish cavities with rice mixture; place fish on capsicums. Roast, covered, 20 minutes. Uncover; roast a further 10 minutes or until fish are cooked as desired.
5 Serve fish on capsicum; accompany with combined orange, spinach and mint.

prep + cook time 1 hour **serves** 4
nutritional count per serving 29g total fat (10.5g saturated fat); 2307kJ (552 cal); 31.5g carbohydrate; 39.3g protein; 5.1g fibre

beef kebabs with roasted vegie salad

1kg (2 pound) piece beef eye fillet,
  chopped coarsely
1½ tablespoons ras el hanout
½ cup (125ml) olive oil
3 large red capsicums (bell peppers) (1kg)
2 medium red onions (340g), cut into wedges
4 cloves garlic, unpeeled
¼ cup (60ml) lemon juice
1 tablespoon finely chopped preserved lemon rind
½ teaspoon ground cumin
500g (1 pound) baby egg (plum) truss tomatoes,
  halved
¼ cup lightly packed fresh coriander (cilantro)
  leaves

1 Combine beef, ras el hanout and half the oil in
large bowl. Cover; refrigerate 3 hours.
2 Quarter capsicums; discard seeds and membranes.
Cook on heated oiled grill plate (or grill or barbecue),
skin-side down, until skin blisters and blackens. Cover
with plastic wrap or paper for 5 minutes; peel away
skin then chop capsicum coarsely.
3 Cook onion and garlic on grill plate until tender;
peel away garlic skin, slice garlic thinly.
4 Combine remaining oil, juice, preserved lemon,
cumin, tomatoes, capsicum, onion and garlic in
large bowl; season to taste.
5 Thread beef onto six metal skewers. Cook skewers
on heated oiled grill plate until cooked as desired.
6 Sprinkle kebabs with coriander; serve with
roasted vegie salad.

prep + cook time 40 minutes (+ refrigeration)
serves 6
nutritional count per serving 27.4g total fat
(6.2g saturated fat); 1898kJ (454 cal);
11g carbohydrate; 38.5g protein; 4.1g fibre

Serve with warm flat bread.

note You could substitute beef rump steak for
the eye fillet, if you prefer.

almond harissa roast lamb

4 cloves garlic, halved
1 tablespoon harissa paste
2 tablespoons coarsely chopped fresh
   flat-leaf parsley
2 large brown onions (600g), sliced thinly
½ cup (125ml) olive oil
½ cup (60g) ground almonds
1.8kg (3¾ pound) leg of lamb

1 Preheat oven to 220°C/425°F.
2 Blend or process garlic, paste, parsley, half the onion and ⅓ cup of the oil until smooth. Transfer mixture to medium bowl, stir in ground almonds.
3 Make deep cuts in lamb to the bone, at 2.5cm (1 inch) intervals. Rub almond mixture all over lamb.
4 Place remaining onion in oiled large baking dish; top with lamb. Drizzle with remaining oil; season. Roast lamb, uncovered, 25 minutes.
5 Reduce oven temperature to 160°C /325°F.
6 Roast lamb a further 1 hour or until cooked as desired. Remove lamb from oven, cover loosely with foil; stand 20 minutes before slicing.

prep + cook time 1 hour 45 minutes (+ standing)
serves 6
nutritional count per serving 38g total fat (9.5g saturated fat); 2424kJ (580 cal); 6.7g carbohydrate; 52.2g protein; 2.8g fibre

minted prawn kebabs

24 uncooked medium king prawns (1kg)
⅓ cup (80ml) lemon juice
¼ cup (60ml) olive oil
2 cloves garlic, crushed
¼ cup finely chopped fresh mint
1 medium lemon (140g), cut into wedges

1 Shell and devein prawns, leaving heads and tails intact. Combine prawns, juice, oil, garlic and mint in large bowl; season. Cover; refrigerate 30 minutes.
2 Thread prawns onto eight metal skewers. Cook skewers on heated oiled grill plate (or grill or barbecue) until prawns are changed in colour.
3 Serve skewers with lemon wedges.

prep + cook time 40 minutes (+ refrigeration)
serves 4
nutritional count per serving 14.6g total fat (2.1g saturated fat); 1028kJ (246 cal); 1.2g carbohydrate; 26.1g protein; 1g fibre

Serve with extra virgin olive oil and sprinkle with fresh mint leaves.

roasted white fish with chermoulla

4 whole baby snapper (1.2kg)
1 teaspoon ground cumin
½ teaspoon hot paprika
2 teaspoons finely grated lemon rind
⅓ cup (80ml) olive oil
⅓ cup each finely chopped fresh coriander (cilantro)
  and flat-leaf parsley
2 tablespoons lemon juice
1 clove garlic, crushed
1 fresh long red chilli, chopped finely

1 Preheat oven to 200°C/400°F.
2 Score fish through thickest part of flesh. Rub fish all over with combined spices, rind and 1 tablespoon of the oil; season.
3 Place fish on oiled oven tray; roast, uncovered, about 25 minutes or until cooked through.
4 Meanwhile, combine remaining oil with remaining ingredients in small bowl; season to taste.
5 Serve fish drizzled with herb mixture.

prep + cook time 35 minutes **serves** 4
nutritional count per serving 20.8g total fat
(3.5g saturated fat); 1346kJ (322 cal);
0.6g carbohydrate; 32.6g protein; 0.6g fibre

Serve with couscous and a green salad.

note Baby bream would also work well in this recipe.

81

spiced lamb roast with figs and honey

3 cloves garlic, chopped finely
4cm (1½ inch) piece fresh ginger (20g), grated
2 fresh long red chillies, chopped finely
⅓ cup each finely chopped fresh coriander (cilantro)
  and flat-leaf parsley
2 teaspoons each ground cumin and coriander
¼ cup (60ml) olive oil
2kg (4 pound) leg of lamb
9 medium fresh figs (540g), halved
2 tablespoons honey

1 Preheat oven to 180°C/350°F.
2 Combine garlic, ginger, chilli, herbs, spices and oil in small bowl.
3 Rub herb mixture all over lamb; season. Place lamb in oiled large baking dish; roast, uncovered, 1¼ hours.
4 Add figs to dish; drizzle honey over figs and lamb. Roast about 15 minutes or until lamb is cooked as desired. Cover lamb; stand 10 minutes before slicing.
5 Serve lamb with figs.

prep + cook time 1 hour 50 minutes serves 6
nutritional count per serving 24.3g total fat (8.4g saturated fat); 2115kJ (506 cal); 15.6g carbohydrate; 55.6g protein; 2.9g fibre

Serve with couscous and a herb salad.

note Make double the herb rub mixture and toss through steamed couscous to make a good accompaniment to the lamb.

lamb kebabs

500g (1 pound) minced (ground) lamb
1 medium brown onion (150g), chopped finely
1 teaspoon each ground cumin and coriander
½ teaspoon each ground ginger, cinnamon
  and hot paprika
¼ cup finely chopped fresh mint
½ cup (140g) yogurt

1 Combine lamb, onion, spices and half the mint in medium bowl; season.
2 Shape lamb mixture into 8 sausages; thread onto 8 bamboo skewers.
3 Cook skewers, in batches, in heated oiled large frying pan until browned and cooked through.
4 Sprinkle skewers with remaining mint; serve with yogurt and lemon wedges.

prep + cook time 45 minutes **serves** 8
nutritional count per serving 10.1g total fat
(4.7g saturated fat); 928kJ (222 cal);
4.2g carbohydrate; 27.9g protein; 0.7g fibre

tip Soak skewers in water for at least an hour before using to prevent burning during cooking.

chicken kebabs with blood orange

4 medium blood oranges (960g)
8 chicken tenderloins (600g)
1 tablespoon moroccan seasoning
¼ cup finely chopped fresh flat-leaf parsley
¼ cup (30g) finely chopped roasted
  unsalted pistachios
1 tablespoon olive oil
1 tablespoon pomegranate molasses
pinch chilli powder

1 Finely grate 2 teaspoons rind from oranges.
2 Combine chicken, seasoning and rind in
medium bowl; season. Thread chicken onto
8 bamboo skewers.
3 Cook skewers on heated oiled grill plate (or grill
or barbecue) until chicken is cooked.
4 Meanwhile, segment oranges over small bowl;
reserve 1 tablespoon juice, chop flesh finely. Combine
orange juice and flesh with remaining ingredients
in small bowl, season to taste.
5 Serve skewers with orange mixture.

prep + cook time 45 minutes **serves** 8
nutritional count per serving 10.9g total fat
(1.8g saturated fat); 1388kJ (332 cal);
19.4g carbohydrate; 36.7g protein; 4.3g fibre

Serve with toasted flatbread.

tip Soak skewers in water for at least an hour before
using to prevent burning during cooking.

slow-roasted spiced lamb shoulder

2 teaspoons fennel seeds
1 teaspoon each ground cinnamon, ginger
  and cumin
¼ teaspoon chilli powder
2 tablespoons olive oil
1.2kg (2½ pound) lamb shoulder, shank intact
2 cloves garlic, sliced thinly
6 baby brown onions (150g)
375g (12 ounces) baby carrots, trimmed
1 cup (250ml) water

1 Preheat oven to 180°C/350°F.
2 Dry-fry spices in small frying pan until fragrant. Combine spices and half the oil in small bowl.
3 Using sharp knife, score lamb at 2.5cm (1 inch) intervals; push garlic into cuts. Rub lamb all over with spice mixture, season.
4 Heat remaining oil in large flameproof dish; cook lamb, turning, until browned all over. Remove lamb from dish.
5 Meanwhile, peel onions, leaving root ends intact. Add onions to dish; cook, stirring, until browned.
6 Add carrots and the water to dish, bring to the boil; top with lamb, cover loosely with foil. Transfer to oven; roast 1½ hours.
7 Reduce oven temperature to 160°C/325°F.
8 Uncover lamb; roast a further 1½ hours or until lamb is tender. Cover lamb; stand 10 minutes, then slice thinly. Strain pan juices into small heatproof jug.
9 Serve lamb with onions, carrots and pan juices.

prep + cook time 3 hours 30 minutes **serves** 4
nutritional count per serving 21.9g total fat
(7.3g saturated fat); 1722kJ (412 cal);
6.5g carbohydrate; 45.7g protein; 3.1g fibre

Serve with steamed green beans.

vegetable dishes

minted carrots with goat's cheese

3 bunches baby carrots (1.2kg), trimmed
2 tablespoons olive oil
2 tablespoons cumin seeds
1 cup firmly packed fresh mint leaves
220g soft goat's cheese, crumbled

1 Combine carrots and oil in large bowl; season.
2 Cook carrots on heated oiled grill plate (or grill or barbecue) about 5 minutes or until tender.
3 Meanwhile, dry-fry seeds in small frying pan until fragrant.
4 Combine carrots, seeds, mint and half the cheese in large bowl; sprinkle with remaining cheese.

prep + cook time 35 minutes **serves** 6
nutritional count per serving 12.1g total fat (4.7g saturated fat); 769kJ (184 cal); 10g carbohydrate; 6.5g protein; 5.6g fibre

note We used an ash-coated cheese in the recipe.

saffron rice with zucchini flowers

12 zucchini flowers, stem attached (240g) (see notes)
45g (1½ ounces) butter
1 large red onion (300g), cut into wedges
2 teaspoons caraway seeds
1 clove garlic, crushed
4 cups (850g) cooked white long-grain rice
  (see notes)
1 teaspoon ground turmeric
pinch saffron threads
¼ cup (20g) flaked almonds, roasted

prep + cook time 30 minutes **serves** 4
nutritional count per serving 12.9g total fat
(6.2g saturated fat); 1747kJ (418 cal);
65.3g carbohydrate; 8g protein; 3.6g fibre

notes The stem of zucchini is the baby zucchini
attached to the flower.
You need to cook about 1½ cups (300g) white
long-grain rice for this recipe. Spread cooked rice
on a flat tray and refrigerate, uncovered, overnight
before using.

1 Remove flowers from zucchini; discard stamens
from flowers. Slice zucchini thinly.
2 Melt butter in large frying pan; cook onion,
seeds and garlic, stirring, until onion softens. Add
sliced zucchini; cook, stirring, until tender. Add rice,
spices and zucchini flowers; cook, stirring, until hot.
Stir in half the nuts; season to taste.
3 Serve sprinkled with remaining nuts.

curried lentils with peas and potato

2 tablespoons olive oil

2 medium potatoes (400g), chopped coarsely

1 medium red onion (170g), chopped finely

2 cloves garlic, crushed

1 tablespoon curry powder

2 cups (500ml) chicken consommé (see note)

15g (½ ounce) butter

800g (30 ounces) canned brown lentils,
  rinsed, drained

2 red banana chillies (250g), seeded, chopped finely

100g (3½ ounces) baby spinach leaves,
  shredded finely

1 cup (120g) frozen peas

1 Heat oil in large frying pan; cook potato, stirring, until browned lightly. Add onion, garlic and curry powder; cook, stirring, until onion softens.

2 Add consommé, butter, lentils, chillies and half the spinach; bring to the boil. Reduce heat; simmer, uncovered, about 15 minutes or until potato is tender.

3 Stir in peas and remaining spinach; simmer, uncovered, until peas are hot. Season to taste.

prep + cook time 40 minutes **serves** 4
nutritional count per serving 13.6g total fat (3.6g saturated fat); 1271kJ (304 cal); 27.3g carbohydrate; 13.4g protein; 9.3g fibre

note Use canned or packaged consommé for a good flavour, but if you prefer, use chicken stock instead.

vegetarian harira

15g (½ ounce) butter
1 large brown onion (200g), chopped finely
2 cloves garlic, crushed
4cm (1½ inch) piece fresh ginger (20g), grated
1 teaspoon ground cinnamon
pinch saffron threads
1 stalk celery (150g), trimmed, chopped finely
1 medium carrot (120g), chopped finely
8 cups (2 litres) water
410g (14 ounces) canned tomato puree
½ cup (100g) brown lentils
½ cup (100g) brown basmati rice
400g (15 ounces) canned chickpeas
  (garbanzo beans), rinsed, drained
2 medium zucchini (240g), chopped finely
3 medium tomatoes (450g), seeded, chopped finely
2 tablespoons lemon juice

1 Melt butter in large saucepan, add onion, garlic and ginger; cook, stirring, until onion softens. Add spices, celery, carrot, the water and puree; bring to the boil. Reduce heat; simmer, uncovered, about 10 minutes or until vegetables are tender.
2 Add lentils, rice and chickpeas; simmer, uncovered, about 20 minutes or until rice and lentils are almost tender. Add zucchini and tomato; simmer, uncovered, about 5 minutes or until zucchini is tender. Remove from heat; stir in juice. Season to taste.

prep + cook time 1 hour **serves** 6
nutritional count per serving 4g total fat
(1.6g saturated fat); 957kJ (229 cal);
33.4g carbohydrate; 10.7g protein; 8.6g fibre

Serve with crusty bread.

note Brown basmati rice is available from most major supermarkets. If it is not available, use white basmati rice instead.

spicy fried potatoes

1kg (2 pounds) baby new potatoes
2 tablespoons olive oil
1 tablespoon harissa paste
2 cloves garlic, crushed
2 teaspoons cumin seeds
2 teaspoons finely grated lemon rind
2 tablespoons finely chopped fresh flat-leaf parsley

1   Boil, steam or microwave potatoes until tender; drain; halve.
2   Heat oil in large frying pan; cook potato, paste, garlic and seeds, stirring occasionally, about 10 minutes or until potato is browned. Stir in rind and parsley; season to taste.

prep + cook time 35 minutes **serves** 6
nutritional count per serving 6.4g total fat (0.9g saturated fat); 732kJ (175 cal); 22.8g carbohydrate; 4.1g protein; 3.8g fibre

baked cabbage with tomatoes

400g (14½ ounces) canned crushed tomatoes
1 small brown onion (80g), grated coarsely
1 clove garlic, crushed
1 teaspoon ground cumin
½ teaspoon white sugar
2 baby green cabbages (800g), quartered
2 tablespoons olive oil
2 tablespoons coarsely chopped fresh
   flat-leaf parsley

1   Preheat oven to 160°C/325°F.
2   Combine undrained tomatoes, onion, garlic, cumin and sugar in small bowl; season to taste.
3   Place cabbage in medium ovenproof dish; top with tomato mixture. Bake, covered, about 30 minutes or until cabbage is tender.
4   Serve cabbage mixture drizzled with oil; sprinkle with parsley.

prep + cook time 40 minutes **serves** 6
nutritional count per serving 6.4g total fat
(0.9g saturated fat); 443kJ (106 cal);
6.7g carbohydrate; 2.8g protein; 5.9g fibre

note If you can't find baby cabbage, use 1 small green cabbage and cut into eight wedges.

chickpea tomato stew

2 tablespoons olive oil
2 medium brown onions (300g), sliced thinly
1 tablespoon light brown sugar
2 teaspoons cumin seeds
1 teaspoon ground coriander
800g (28 ounces) canned whole tomatoes
1 cup (250ml) vegetable stock
800g (30 ounces) canned chickpeas
  (garbanzo beans), rinsed, drained
1 cup (150g) raisins
⅓ cup (70g) coarsely chopped preserved
  lemon rind
60g (2 ounces) baby spinach leaves

1 Heat oil in flameproof tagine or large saucepan; cook onion and sugar over low heat, stirring occasionally, about 15 minutes or until onions are lightly caramelised. Add spices; cook, stirring, about 1 minute or until mixture is fragrant.
2 Add undrained tomatoes, stock, chickpeas, raisins and lemon; bring to the boil. Reduce heat; simmer, covered, about 30 minutes or until thickened slightly. Stir in spinach; season to taste.

prep + cook time 1 hour **serves** 6
nutritional count per serving 8.7g total fat
(1.3g saturated fat); 1195kJ (286 cal);
39.7g carbohydrate; 8.7g protein; 8.5g fibre

desserts & pastries

saffron panna cotta with honeyed figs

1 cup (250ml) pouring cream
½ cup (110g) caster (superfine) sugar
pinch saffron threads
8 cardamom pods, bruised
2 cinnamon sticks
4 teaspoons gelatine
2 tablespoons water
2 cups (500ml) buttermilk
HONEYED FIGS
¼ cup (90g) honey
¼ cup (60ml) dry red wine
⅓ cup (65g) finely chopped dried figs

1 Combine cream, sugar and spices in medium saucepan; stir over low heat until sugar dissolves. Bring to the boil. Strain mixture into large heatproof jug; cool 5 minutes.
2 Meanwhile, sprinkle gelatine over the water in small heatproof jug. Stand jug in small saucepan of simmering water; stir until gelatine dissolves, cool 5 minutes.
3 Stir gelatine mixture and buttermilk into cream mixture. Divide mixture into six ¾-cup (180ml) moulds. Cover; refrigerate 4 hours or until set.
4 Make honeyed figs.
5 Turn panna cottas onto serving plates; top with honeyed figs.
HONEYED FIGS Combine ingredients in medium saucepan; bring to the boil. Reduce heat; simmer, uncovered, about 5 minutes or until syrup thickens slightly. Cool.

prep + cook time 30 minutes (+ refrigeration)
serves 6
nutritional count per serving 19.8g total fat (13g saturated fat); 1576kJ (377 cal); 42.4g carbohydrate; 6.7g protein; 1.5g fibre

Serve with almond bread.

99

hazelnut and date tart

1 sheet shortcrust pastry
125g (4 ounces) butter, softened
⅓ cup (75g) caster (superfine) sugar
2 tablespoons finely grated lemon rind
2 eggs
1 cup (100g) ground hazelnuts
1 tablespoon plain (all-purpose) flour
1 teaspoon ground cinnamon
½ cup (60g) seeded dried dates, halved lengthways
½ cup (180g) honey, warmed
SESAME CREAM
1¼ cups (310ml) thickened (heavy) cream
  (see notes)
2 tablespoons caster (superfine) sugar
2 teaspoons black sesame seeds
1 teaspoon vanilla extract
1 teaspoon sesame oil

1 Preheat oven to 200°C/400°F.
2 Line greased 24cm-round loose-based flan tin with pastry; press into base and sides, trim edge. Refrigerate 30 minutes.
3 Meanwhile, beat butter, sugar and rind in small bowl with electric mixer until combined. Beat in eggs, one at a time. Stir in ground hazelnuts, flour and cinnamon.
4 Spread hazelnut filling into pastry case; top with dates. Bake about 35 minutes or until firm. Brush hot tart with half the honey. Cool in tin.
5 Meanwhile, make sesame cream.
6 Serve tart drizzled with remaining honey; top with sesame cream.
SESAME CREAM Beat cream and sugar in small bowl with electric mixer until soft peaks form; fold in remaining ingredients.

prep + cook time 55 minutes
(+ refrigeration and cooling) **serves** 8
nutritional count per serving 42.6g total fat (21.5g saturated fat); 2508kJ (600 cal); 49.4g carbohydrate; 6.5g protein; 2.6g fibre

notes It is fine to use 1 x 300ml container of thickened cream for this recipe.
You can use ready-ground almonds (also known as almond meal), available from supermarkets and health-food stores, rather than grounding your own hazelnuts.
Black sesame seeds are available from specialty spice shops.

pastilla with sweet yogurt cream

90g (3 ounces) unsalted butter
1 tablespoon each honey and maple syrup
5 sheets fillo pastry
½ cup (65g) finely chopped roasted
  unsalted pistachios
SWEET YOGURT CREAM
250g (8 ounces) mascarpone cheese
1 tablespoon caster (superfine) sugar
½ cup (125g) sheep's-milk yogurt
1 tablespoon finely grated lemon rind
50g chocolate-coated honeycomb bar,
  chopped finely

1 Preheat oven to 200°C/400°F. Grease and line two oven trays.
2 Combine butter, honey and maple syrup in small saucepan; stir over low heat until smooth.
3 To make pastilla, brush 1 sheet of pastry with butter mixture, sprinkle with some of the nuts; top with another pastry sheet. Repeat layering with remaining pastry, butter mixture and nuts. Cut layered sheets into 24 squares; place on oven trays.
4 Bake pastilla about 10 minutes or until crisp; transfer to wire rack to cool.
5 Meanwhile, make sweet yogurt cream. Serve pastilla with yogurt cream.
SWEET YOGURT CREAM Beat cheese and sugar in small bowl with electric mixer until smooth; fold in yogurt, rind and honeycomb bar.

prep + cook time 35 minutes serves 6
nutritional count per serving 43.9g total fat (26.1g saturated fat); 2144 kJ (513 cal); 25.6g carbohydrate; 5.2g protein; 1.4g fibre

note Sweet pastilla is traditionally served with sweetened warmed milk to reduce the crunchiness of the layered pastille. We like to use the pastilla to dip into the sweet yogurt cream.

m'hanncha

90g (3 ounces) butter, melted
1⅔ cups (200g) ground almonds
½ teaspoon almond extract
½ cup (80g) icing (confectioners') sugar
2 teaspoons rosewater
45g (1½ ounces) dark eating chocolate,
  grated coarsely
6 sheets fillo pastry
75g (2½ ounces) butter, melted, extra
1 egg, beaten lightly
½ teaspoon ground cinnamon

1   Preheat oven to 160°C/325°F. Grease 20cm (8 inch) springform tin.
2   Combine butter, ground almonds, extract, sifted icing sugar, rosewater and chocolate in medium bowl. Roll rounded teaspoons of mixture into balls. Roll balls into 2.5cm (1 inch) log shapes.
3   Brush 1 sheet of pastry with some of the extra butter; top with a second pastry sheet, brush with butter. Place one-third of the chocolate logs along one long end, 5cm (2 inches) from edge, leaving 2.5cm (1 inch) border on short ends. Roll pastry tightly to enclose logs. Repeat with remaining pastry, butter and logs. Brush pastry logs with butter.
4   Pinch one end of one pastry log to seal – this will become the centre of the spiral. Wind the pastry log into a tight spiral, brushing with egg to join. Continue adding pastry logs, end-to-end, in spiral pattern, brushing with egg to join and seal ends. Transfer spiral to tin. Brush with egg, sprinkle with cinnamon. Bake about 25 minutes or until golden.
5   Serve dusted with a little sifted icing sugar.

prep + cook time 55 minutes **serves** 8
nutritional count per serving 33.3g total fat (13.3g saturated fat); 1710kJ (409 cal); 20.5g carbohydrate; 7.4g protein; 2.5g fibre

note M'hanncha, a Moroccan almond pastry, means 'the snake' and this coiled sweet pastry treat certainly represents that. However, instead of running away, our delicious chocolate almond recipe will have everyone running back for more.

watermelon and fig salad

1.2kg (2½ pound) piece seedless watermelon
6 medium fresh figs (360g), sliced into rounds
¾ cup (200g) greek-style yogurt
1 teaspoon rosewater
¼ cup loosely packed fresh small mint leaves
⅓ cup (35g) roasted walnuts, chopped finely

1 Cut away skin and white pith from melon; cut melon into thin wedges. Arrange melon and figs on large platter.
2 Combine yogurt and rosewater in small bowl; drizzle over fruit. Sprinkle with mint and nuts.

prep time 15 minutes **serves** 4
nutritional count per serving 10.2g total fat (2.7g saturated fat); 882kJ (211 cal); 21.8g carbohydrate; 5.9g protein; 4.2g fibre

ghoriba biscuits

90g (3 ounces) butter, melted
3 eggs
1¼ cups (200g) icing (confectioners') sugar
1¼ cups (200g) fine semolina flour
1½ cups (225g) self-raising flour
1 teaspoon vanilla extract
1 teaspoon orange blossom water
2 tablespoons pure icing sugar, extra

1 Preheat oven to 160°C/325°F. Line greased oven trays with baking paper.
2 Combine butter, eggs and sifted icing sugar in large bowl. Stir in semolina, sifted flour, extract and orange blossom water.
3 Roll level tablespoons of mixture into balls, place about 7cm apart on trays; flatten slightly. Sift extra icing sugar over biscuits. Bake about 15 minutes or until biscuits are golden and sugar has 'cracked'. cool on wire rack.

prep + cook time 35 minutes **makes** 30
nutritional count per biscuit 3.2g total fat
(1.8g saturated fat); 443kJ (106 cal);
17.1g carbohydrate; 2.2g protein; 0.5g fibre

spiced oranges with brown sugar toffee

1 cup (220g) firmly packed light brown sugar
1 cup (250ml) water
3 medium oranges (720g), peeled, sliced thickly
3 medium blood oranges (500g), peeled,
  sliced thickly
¼ teaspoon ground cinnamon
pinch ground cardamom
1 teaspoon orange blossom water

1 Stir sugar and the water in medium saucepan over medium heat until sugar dissolves; bring to the boil. Boil, uncovered, without stirring, about 10 minutes or until mixture is a dark caramel colour. Remove from heat; allow bubbles to subside.
2 Meanwhile, arrange orange slices, overlapping slightly, on large heatproof platter; sprinkle with spices and orange blossom water.
3 Pour half the toffee over oranges; pour remaining toffee onto greased oven tray. Stand oranges at room temperature about 2 hours or until toffee dissolves and forms a sauce over oranges. Allow toffee on tray to set at room temperature.
4 Break set toffee into pieces; sprinkle over oranges.

prep + cook time 25 minutes (+ standing) serves 6
nutritional count per serving 0.1g total fat
(0g saturated fat); 815kJ (195 cal);
46.9g carbohydrate; 1.5g protein; 2.9g fibre

tip When you think the syrup has almost reached the colour we suggest, quickly remove the pan from the heat, remembering that the syrup will continue to cook and darken during this time. Let the bubbles subside, then drop a teaspoon of the syrup into a cup of cold water. The toffee should set the instant it hits the cold water; lift it out and break it with your fingers. If the toffee needs to be harder, then return the mixture to the heat and cook a little more. This test is easy, but a candy thermometer removes all the guess work for you. If you have a candy thermometer, boil the mixture until it reaches 138°C/280°F.

almond rice pudding

1.5 litres (6 cups) milk
2 cups (320g) blanched almonds
¼ cup (55g) caster (superfine) sugar
5cm strip orange rind
⅔ cup (130g) arborio rice
½ teaspoon orange blossom water
1 large pomegranate (430g)
¼ cup (35g) roasted slivered almonds
pinch ground cinnamon

1 Blend milk and blanched nuts, in batches, until smooth. Strain milk mixture through fine sieve into large saucepan.
2 Stir sugar and rind into milk mixture over high heat; bring to the boil, stirring occasionally.
3 Gradually stir in rice. Reduce heat; simmer, uncovered, over low heat, stirring occasionally, about 35 minutes or until rice is tender. Discard rind; stir in orange blossom water. Stand 10 minutes.
4 Remove seeds from pomegranate; serve warm rice sprinkled with seeds, slivered nuts and cinnamon.

prep + cook time 1 hour (+ standing) **serves** 6
nutritional count per serving 42.8g total fat
(8.4g saturated fat); 2730kJ (653 cal);
43.5g carbohydrate; 22.4g protein; 6.8g fibre

charosets

10 fresh dates (200g), seeded, chopped coarsely
½ cup (70g) raisins
½ cup (55g) coarsely chopped roasted walnuts
1½ tablespoons sweet red wine
200g (6½ ounces) dark eating chocolate
  (70% cocoa solids), melted
⅓ cup (40g) finely chopped roasted walnuts

1 Blend or process dates, raisins, coarsely chopped nuts and wine until mixture forms a smooth paste.
2 Using wet hands, roll level teaspoons of mixture into balls; place on baking (parchment) paper lined tray. Cover; refrigerate overnight.
3 Dip half the balls in melted chocolate, place on foil-lined tray; leave to set at room temperature. Roll remaining balls in finely chopped nuts.

prep time 30 minutes (+ refrigeration) **makes** 50
nutritional count per charoset 2.5g total fat
(0.8g saturated fat); 176kJ (42 cal);
4.4g carbohydrate; 0.5g protein; 0.4g fibre

gazelles horns

180g (6 ounces) butter, softened
⅔ cup (110g) icing (confectioners') sugar
2 eggs
2⅔ cups (400g) plain (all-purpose) flour
1 tablespoon orange blossom water
2 teaspoons iced water, approximately
1 tablespoon milk
½ cup (80g) icing (confectioners') sugar, extra
1 teaspoon ground cinnamon
ALMOND FILLING
2 cups (240g) ground almonds
½ cup (80g) icing (confectioners') sugar
1 egg
45g (1½ ounces) butter, melted
1 tablespoon orange blossom water

1 Beat butter and sifted icing sugar in medium bowl with electric mixer until smooth. Beat in eggs, one at a time. Stir in sifted flour, orange blossom water and enough of the water to make a firm dough. Divide dough in half; cover, refrigerate 30 minutes.
2 Meanwhile, make almond filling.
3 Preheat oven to 160°C/325°F. Grease and line oven trays.
4 Roll each dough half, separately, between sheets of baking (parchment) paper until 2mm thick; cut 20 x 7.5cm (3 inch) rounds from each sheet of dough. Re-roll scraps of dough, if necessary, to make a total of 40 rounds.
5 Drop rounded teaspoons of almond filling into centre of rounds; brush edges with a little water. Fold rounds in half, press edges with a fork to seal. Pinch ends slightly to create horn shapes. Place horns on oven trays; brush with milk. Bake about 20 minutes or until browned lightly.
6 Roll warm horns in combined extra sifted icing sugar and cinnamon. Serve horns warm or cold.
ALMOND FILLING Combine ingredients in medium bowl.

prep + cook time 1 hour (+ refrigeration) **makes** 40
nutritional count per horn 8.5g total fat
(3.4g saturated fat); 606kJ (145 cal);
14.3g carbohydrate; 2.9g protein; 0.9g fibre

spiced crème caramel

¾ cup (165g) caster (superfine) sugar
½ cup (125ml) water
1¼ cups (310ml) pouring cream (see note)
1¾ cups (430ml) milk
4 cardamom pods, bruised
¼ teaspoon saffron threads
2 teaspoons rosewater
6 eggs
⅓ cup (75g) caster (superfine) sugar, extra

1 Stir sugar and the water in medium frying pan over medium heat until sugar dissolves; bring to the boil. Boil, uncovered, without stirring, until mixture is a dark caramel colour. Remove from heat; allow bubbles to subside. Pour toffee into deep 20cm (8 inch) round cake pan.
2 Combine cream, milk, spices and rosewater in medium saucepan; bring to the boil. Remove from heat; stand 30 minutes, then return to the boil.
3 Whisk eggs and extra sugar in medium bowl; whisking constantly, pour hot milk mixture into egg mixture. Strain mixture into cake pan; discard solids.
4 Meanwhile, preheat oven to 160°C/325°F.
5 Place pan in medium baking dish; add enough boiling water to come half way up side of pan. Bake crème caramel about 40 minutes or until set. Remove pan from baking dish. Cover crème caramel; refrigerate overnight.
6 Gently ease crème caramel from side of pan; invert onto deep-sided serving plate.

prep + cook time 1 hour
(+ standing and refrigeration) **serves** 6
nutritional count per serving 30.4g total fat
(18g saturated fat); 2027kJ (485 cal);
45.1g carbohydrate; 10.9g protein; 0g fibre

note It is fine to use 1 x 300ml carton of cream for this recipe.

rosewater and orange couscous

1 medium orange (240g)
1½ cups (375ml) water
⅓ cup (75g) caster (superfine) sugar
1½ cups (300g) couscous
30g (1 ounce) butter
1 teaspoon rosewater
½ teaspoon ground cinnamon
⅓ cup (65g) finely chopped dried figs
⅓ cup (45g) coarsely chopped roasted
  unsalted pistachios
⅔ cup (190g) yogurt
¼ cup loosely packed fresh mint leaves

1   Finely grate 2 teaspoons rind from orange.
Segment orange over small bowl.
2   Stir the water and sugar in small saucepan over
medium heat until sugar dissolves; bring to the boil.
3   Combine couscous with the sugar syrup mixture,
butter, rosewater, cinnamon and rind in medium
heatproof bowl, cover; stand about 5 minutes or
until liquid is absorbed, fluffing with fork occasionally.
Stir figs and half the nuts into couscous.
4   Serve couscous topped with orange segments
and yogurt; sprinkle with remaining nuts and mint.

prep + cook time 25 minutes (+ standing) serves 4
nutritional count per serving 13.5g total fat
(5.5g saturated fat); 2362kJ (565 cal);
93.1g carbohydrate; 15.4g protein; 5.1g fibre

note Use your favourite thick yogurt; sheep's-milk
yogurt is delicious in this recipe.

glossary

ALMONDS flat, pointy-ended nuts with pitted brown shells enclosing a creamy white kernel covered by a brown skin.
blanched nuts with skins removed.
flaked paper-thin slices.
ground also known as almond meal; nuts are powdered to a flour-like texture.
slivered small lengthways-cut pieces.

ARTICHOKE HEARTS tender centre of the globe artichoke; purchased in brine, canned or in glass jars.

BASIL an aromatic herb; there are many types, but the most commonly used is sweet, or common, basil.

BEANS
broad also known as fava, windsor and horse beans; available dried, fresh, canned and frozen. Fresh and frozen forms should be peeled twice discarding both the outer long green pod and the beige-green tough inner shell.
cannellini small white bean similar in appearance and flavour to haricot, navy and great northern, all of which can be substituted for each other.
green also known as french or string beans (although the tough string they once had has generally been bred out of them); this long thin fresh bean is consumed in its entirety once cooked.

BEEF
chuck steak comes from the neck and shoulder of the beef, and tends to be chewy but flavourful and inexpensive. A good cut for braising or stewing.
eye fillet a very tender cut from the area below the rib cage; also known as beef tenderloin.

BEETROOT also known as red beets or beets; a firm, round root vegetable.

BLOOD ORANGE a virtually seedless citrus fruit with a reddish rind and flesh; has a sweet, non-acidic pulp and the juice has slight strawberry or raspberry tones.

BREADCRUMBS, STALE one- or two-day-old bread made into crumbs by blending or processing.

BUTTER use salted or unsalted (sweet) butter; 125g is equal to one stick (4 ounces) of butter.

CAPSICUM also known as bell pepper or, simply, pepper. Comes in many colours: red, green, yellow, orange and purplish-black. Be sure to discard the seeds and membranes before use.

roasted capsicum available loose from delis or packed in jars in oil or brine.

CAYENNE PEPPER long, thin-fleshed, extremely hot red chilli usually sold dried and ground.

CHEESE
goat's made from goat's milk, has an earthy, strong taste; available in both soft and firm textures, in various shapes and sizes, sometimes rolled in ash or herbs.
mascarpone an unripened, smooth, fresh, triple cream cheese with a rich, sweet, slightly acidic, taste.

CHICKEN
drumsticks leg with skin and bone intact.
tenderloins thin tender strip of meat lying just under the breast.
thigh cutlets thigh with skin and centre bone intact; sometimes found skinned.
thigh fillets thigh with the skin and bone removed.

CHICKPEAS also called garbanzos, channa or hummus; irregularly round, sandy-coloured legume.

CHILLI available in many different types and sizes. Use rubber gloves when seeding and chopping fresh chillies as they can burn your skin. Removing seeds and membranes lessens the heat level.
banana chillies can be pale olive green, yellow and red in colour. Available from greengrocers and larger supermarkets.
flakes deep-red, dehydrated chilli slices and whole seeds.
long red available both fresh and dried; a generic term used for any moderately hot, long (6cm-8cm), thin chilli.
powder the Asian variety, made from dried ground thai chillies, is the hottest; it can be used as a substitute for fresh chillies in the proportion of ½ teaspoon ground chilli powder to 1 medium chopped fresh chilli.
red thai a small, hot, bright red chilli.

CHOCOLATE
dark eating also known as semi-sweet or luxury chocolate; made of a high percentage of cocoa liquor, cocoa butter and a little added sugar. We use dark eating chocolate unless stated otherwise.
chocolate-coated honeycomb bar a honeycomb confectionery covered in milk chocolate.

CONSOMMÉ a clear soup usually of beef, veal or chicken.

CORIANDER also known as pak chee, cilantro or chinese parsley; bright-green leafy herb with a pungent flavour. Both the stems and roots of coriander are also used in cooking; wash well before using. Also available ground or as seeds; these should not be substituted for the fresh herb as the tastes are completely different.

COUSCOUS a fine grain-like cereal product made from semolina; a dough of semolina flour and water is sieved then dehydrated to produce minuscule even-sized pellets of couscous; it is rehydrated by steaming, or with the addition of a warm liquid, and swells to three or four times its original size.

CREAM we use fresh cream also known as pure cream and pouring cream. It has a minimum fat content of 35%.

CUCUMBER
lebanese thin-skinned, short and slender. Probably the most popular variety because of its tender, edible skin, tiny, yielding seeds and sweet, fresh and flavoursome taste.
telegraph also known as the european or burpless cucumber; slender and long (35cm), its thin dark-green skin has shallow ridges running down its length.

CURRANTS, DRIED these tiny, almost black raisins are so-named after a grape variety originating in Corinth, Greece.

DATES fruit of the date palm tree; are green when unripe and turn yellow, golden brown, black or mahogany red, depending on the variety, as they ripen. About 4cm-6cm in length, plump and oval, thin-skinned, with a honey-sweet flavour and sticky texture. Available fresh or dried, pitted or unpitted.

EGGPLANT also known as aubergine.
baby also known as finger or japanese eggplant; very small and slender so can be used without disgorging.

FENNEL also known as finocchio or anise; a white to very pale green-white, firm, crisp, roundish vegetable about 8cm-12cm in diameter. The bulb has a slightly sweet, anise flavour, but the leaves have a much stronger taste. Also the name given to dried seeds having a licorice flavour.

FIGS vary in skin and flesh colour according to type not ripeness. When ripe, figs should be unblemished and bursting with flesh; nectar beads at the base indicate when a fig is at its best.

FILLO PASTRY also known as phyllo; tissue-thin pastry sheets purchased chilled or frozen.

FLOUR
plain an all-purpose flour made from wheat.
self-raising plain flour sifted with baking powder in the proportion of 1 cup flour to 2 teaspoons baking powder.

GELATINE a thickening agent; we use powdered gelatine. It is also available in sheet form, known as leaf gelatine.

GINGER also known as green or root ginger; the thick root of a tropical plant.

HARISSA a Moroccan sauce or paste made from dried chillies, cumin, garlic, oil and caraway seeds. The paste, available in a tube, is very hot and should not be used in large amounts; bottled harissa sauce is more mild. From supermarkets and Middle-Eastern grocery stores.

KUMARA (orange sweet potato) Polynesian name of an orange-fleshed sweet potato often confused with yam.

LEEK a member of the onion family; resembles a green onion, but is much larger and more subtle and mild in flavour.

LEMON THYME a herb with a lemony scent, which is due to the high level of citral in its leaves – an oil also found in lemon, orange, verbena and lemon grass. The citrus scent is enhanced by crushing the leaves in your hands before using the herb.

LENTILS (red, brown, yellow) dried pulses often identified by and named after their colour.

MARJORAM closely related to oregano; its flavour is distinctive but sweeter and milder than oregano and tastes slightly earthy.

MINCE also known as ground meat.

OIL
avocado is pressed from the flesh of the avocado fruit. Has a high smoke point. It is high in monounsaturated fats and vitamin E.
mustard seed is rich and full-bodied with a buttery, nutty flavour, but without the heat or strong mustard taste. Cold-pressed oil is pressed from the whole seed, with no heat treatment, and is then filtered and bottled. It has a low saturated fat content and is high in omega-3 and monounsaturated fats.

olive made from ripened olives. Extra virgin and virgin are the best, while extra light or light refers to taste not fat levels.
sesame made from roasted, crushed, white sesame seeds; a flavouring rather than a cooking medium.
vegetable sourced from plants rather than animal fats.

OLIVES
black have a richer and more mellow flavour than the green ones and are softer in texture. Sold either plain or in a piquant marinade.
green those harvested before fully ripened and are, as a rule, denser and more bitter than their black relatives.
rainbow cerignola olives, grown in Italy, are large oval-shaped olives that can be either black or bright green in colour, depending on maturity. They may also come in a variety of colours, including yellow, red, green and brown; the colour depends on the curing medium – brine, lye or salt. Available from speciality food stores and delicatessens.

ONIONS
baby brown are also known as cocktail onions and pickling onions; larger than shallots they are used raw, pickled in brine, or cooked in stews and casseroles.
green also known as scallion or, incorrectly, shallot; an immature onion picked before the bulb has formed, having a long, bright-green edible stalk.
red also known as spanish, red spanish or bermuda onion; a sweet-flavoured, large, purple-red onion.
shallots also called french shallots, golden shallots or eschalots; small, brown-skinned, elongated members of the onion family. Grows in tight clusters similar to garlic.
spring these onions have small white bulbs, long green leaves with narrow green-leafed tops.

ORANGE BLOSSOM WATER also known as orange flower water; a concentrated flavouring made from orange blossoms. Available from Middle-Eastern food stores and some supermarkets and delicatessens. Cannot be substituted with citrus flavourings, as the taste is completely different.

OREGANO also known as wild marjoram; has a woody stalk with clumps of tiny, dark green leaves that have a pungent, peppery flavour. Used fresh or dried.

PARSLEY, FLAT-LEAF also known as continental parsley or italian parsley.

PATTY PAN SQUASH also known as crookneck or custard marrow pumpkins; a round, slightly flat summer squash being yellow to pale-green in colour and having a scalloped edge. Harvested young, it has a firm white flesh and distinct flavour.

PEPITAS dried pumpkin seeds.

PISTACHIOS pale green, delicately flavoured nuts inside hard off-white shells. To peel, soak shelled nuts in boiling water for about 5 minutes; drain, then pat dry with absorbent paper. Rub skins with cloth to peel. Our recipes give the amount of shelled nuts required.

POMEGRANATE MOLASSES is thicker, browner and more concentrated in flavour than grenadine, the sweet, red pomegranate syrup used in cocktails. Possesses tart and fruity qualities similar to balsamic vinegar. It is available from Middle-Eastern food stores, specialty food shops and better delicatessens.

POTATOES, BABY NEW also known as chats; not a separate variety but an early harvest with very thin skin.

PRESERVED LEMON RIND a North African specialty; lemons are quartered and preserved in salt and lemon juice or water. To use, remove and discard pulp, squeeze juice from rind, rinse rind well; slice thinly. Sold in jars by delicatessens and some larger supermarkets; once opened, store under refrigeration.

PRUNES commercially or sun-dried plums.

QUINCE yellow-skinned fruit with a hard texture and astringent, tart taste; eaten cooked or as a preserve. Long, slow cooking turns the flesh a deep rose pink. Is related to the apple and pear.

RADISH a peppery root vegetable related to the mustard plant. The small round red variety is the mildest; it is crisp and juicy, and usually eaten raw in salads.

RAISINS dried sweet grapes.

RICE
arborio small, round-grain rice well suited to absorb a large amount of liquid.
basmati a white, fragrant, long-grained rice. Wash several times before cooking.
brown basmati has more fibre and a stronger flavour than the white variety, but takes twice as long to cook.

medium-grain previously sold as calrose rice; extremely versatile rice that can be substituted for short- or long-grain rices.

ROCKET also known as arugula, rugula and rucola; a peppery-tasting green leaf that can be used similarly to baby spinach leaves. Baby rocket leaves, also known as wild rocket, are smaller and less peppery.

ROSEWATER this is distilled from rose petals, and is used in the Middle East, North Africa and India to flavour desserts. Don't confuse with rose essence, which is more concentrated.

RUBY RED GRAPEFRUIT pink fleshed grapefruit; not as tart as the yellow variety.

SEAFOOD

prawns also known as shrimp. Varieties include, school, king, royal red, sydney harbour, tiger. Can be bought uncooked (green) or cooked, with or without shells.

snapper a saltwater fish. Some of the better-known species include the gray, mutton, schoolmaster and yellowtail. Red snapper, the most popular, is so-named because of its reddish-pink skin and red eyes. Its flesh is firm textured and contains very little fat.

trout a delicately-flavoured fish that belongs to the same family as salmon; classified as an oily fish. Most trout are freshwater, but some are saltwater. There are a number of different types including sea trout, rainbow trout and brown trout.

tuna reddish with a slightly dry, firm flesh. Many varieties are available including bluefin, yellowfin, skipjack or albacore; substitute with swordfish.

white fish fillets, firm blue eye, bream, flathead, swordfish, ling, whiting, jewfish or snapper are all good choices. Check for any small pieces of bone and use tweezers to remove them.

SEMOLINA is made from durum wheat milled into various textured granules, all of these are finer than flour; it is available from health-food stores and some major supermarkets. Semolina can be replaced (weight for weight) with plain flour.

SILVER BEET also known as swiss chard and, mistakenly, spinach; a member of the beet family grown for its tasty green leaves and celery-like stems. Also known as blettes.

SPICES

anise also known as aniseed or sweet cumin, related to parsley. The seeds have a mildly sweet licorice flavour.

caraway seeds a member of the parsley family; also available in ground form. Has a pungent aroma and a distinctly sweet but tangy flavour.

cardamom can be purchased in pod, seed or ground form. Has a distinctive aromatic, sweetly rich flavour and is one of the world's most expensive spices.

cinnamon dried inner bark of the shoots of the cinnamon tree; available in stick (quill) or ground form.

coriander seeds have a mild, lemon-like taste that compliments both sweet and savoury dishes. Ground coriander seeds are found in sweet mixed spice blends for cakes and biscuits as well as being used to thicken and flavour curries. Indian coriander seeds are pale green and have a flavour that is reminiscent of fresh coriander leaf.

cumin also known as zeera or comino; has a spicy, nutty flavour.

dukkah an Egyptian spice blend made of roasted nuts and aromatic spices. It is available from Middle-Eastern food stores, specialty spice stores and some larger supermarkets.

ginger also known as powdered ginger; used as a flavouring in cakes, pies and puddings but cannot be substituted for fresh ginger.

moroccan seasoning is available from most Middle-Eastern food stores, spice shops and major supermarkets. Turmeric, cinnamon and cumin add authentic Moroccan flavouring to dishes.

nutmeg the dried nut of an evergreen tree native to Indonesia; it is available in ground form, or you can grate your own with a fine grater.

paprika a ground, dried, sweet red capsicum (bell pepper); there are many types available, including sweet, hot, mild and smoked.

ras el hanout is a classic spice blend used in Moroccan cooking. The name means 'top of the shop' and is the very best spice blend that a spice merchant has to offer. The blends may often contain more than 20 different spices.

saffron comes from the dried stigmas of the saffron crocus; it takes 225,000 hand-picked stigmas to make a half a kilo (500g), which explains why it is the world's most expensive spice. Imparts a yellow-orange colour to food when infused.

turmeric a member of the ginger family, the dried, ground root adds a rich yellow colour to dishes. It is pungent but not hot.

za'atar a blend of roasted sesame seeds, sumac and crushed dried herbs such as wild marjoram and thyme, its content is largely determined by the individual maker. Used to flavour many familiar Middle Eastern dishes, pizza and savoury pastries; available in delicatessens and specialty food stores.

SPINACH also known as english spinach and, incorrectly, silver beet. Baby spinach is also available.

SUGAR

brown extremely soft, finely granulated sugar retaining molasses for its colour and flavour.

caster also known as superfine or finely granulated table sugar.

icing sugar also known as confectioners' or powdered sugar; granulated sugar crushed together with a small amount of cornflour.

pure icing sugar also known as confectioners' sugar or powdered sugar, but has no added cornflour.

raw natural brown granulated sugar.

white coarse, granulated table sugar, also known as crystal sugar.

TOMATOES

cherry also known as tiny tim or tom thumb tomatoes; small and round.

paste triple-concentrated tomato puree.

semi-dried partially dried tomato pieces in olive oil; softer and juicier than sun-dried, these are not a preserve, so do not keep as long as sun-dried.

truss small vine-ripened tomatoes with the vine still attached.

VANILLA EXTRACT made by extracting the flavour from the vanilla bean pod; the pods are soaked, usually in alcohol, to capture the authentic flavour.

VINEGAR

red wine based on fermented red wine.

white wine is made from a blend of white wines.

WATERCRESS also known as winter rocket. Is a member of the cress family, a large group of peppery greens. Highly perishable, so must be used as soon as possible after purchase.

ZUCCHINI also known as courgette; small, pale- or dark-green, yellow or white vegetable belonging to the squash family. Harvested when young, its edible flowers can be stuffed then deep-fried or oven-baked to make delicious appetisers.

conversion chart

MEASURES

One Australian metric measuring cup holds approximately 250ml; one Australian metric tablespoon holds 20ml; one Australian metric teaspoon holds 5ml.

The difference between one country's measuring cups and another's is within a two- or three-teaspoon variance, and will not affect your cooking results. North America, New Zealand and the United Kingdom use a 15ml tablespoon.

All cup and spoon measurements are level. The most accurate way of measuring dry ingredients is to weigh them. When measuring liquids, use a clear glass or plastic jug with the metric markings.

We use large eggs with an average weight of 60g.

DRY MEASURES

METRIC	IMPERIAL
15g	½oz
30g	1oz
60g	2oz
90g	3oz
125g	4oz (¼lb)
155g	5oz
185g	6oz
220g	7oz
250g	8oz (½lb)
280g	9oz
315g	10oz
345g	11oz
375g	12oz (¾lb)
410g	13oz
440g	14oz
470g	15oz
500g	16oz (1lb)
750g	24oz (1½lb)
1kg	32oz (2lb)

LIQUID MEASURES

METRIC	IMPERIAL
30ml	1 fluid oz
60ml	2 fluid oz
100ml	3 fluid oz
125ml	4 fluid oz
150ml	5 fluid oz
190ml	6 fluid oz
250ml	8 fluid oz
300ml	10 fluid oz
500ml	16 fluid oz
600ml	20 fluid oz
1000ml (1 litre)	1¾ pints

LENGTH MEASURES

METRIC	IMPERIAL
3mm	⅛in
6mm	¼in
1cm	½in
2cm	¾in
2.5cm	1in
5cm	2in
6cm	2½in
8cm	3in
10cm	4in
13cm	5in
15cm	6in
18cm	7in
20cm	8in
23cm	9in
25cm	10in
28cm	11in
30cm	12in (1ft)

OVEN TEMPERATURES

The oven temperatures in this book are for conventional ovens; if you have a fan-forced oven, decrease the temperature by 10-20 degrees.

	°C (CELSIUS)	°F (FAHRENHEIT)
Very slow	120	250
Slow	150	300
Moderately slow	160	325
Moderate	180	350
Moderately hot	200	400
Hot	220	425
Very hot	240	475

index

Published in 2010 by ACP Books, Sydney
ACP Books are published by ACP Magazines
a division of PBL Media Pty Limited

ACP BOOKS

General manager Christine Whiston
Editor-in-chief Susan Tomnay
Creative director & designer Hieu Chi Nguyen
Art director Hannah Blackmore
Design assistant Sarah Holmes
Senior editor Wendy Bryant
Food director Pamela Clark
Sales & rights director Brian Cearnes
Marketing manager Bridget Cody
Senior business analyst Rebecca Varela
Circulation manager Jarna Mclean
Operations manager David Scotto
Production manager Victoria Jefferys

Published by ACP Books, a division of ACP Magazines Ltd,
54 Park St, Sydney; GPO Box 4088, Sydney, NSW 2001.
phone (02) 9282 8618; fax (02) 9267 9438.

acpbooks@acpmagazines.com.au; www.acpbooks.com.au

Printed by Toppan Printing Co, China.

United Kingdom Distributed by Australian Consolidated Press (UK),
phone (01604) 642 200; fax (01604) 642 300; books@acpuk.com

Title: Moroccan / food director Pamela Clark.
ISBN: 978 1 86396 940 6 (pbk.)
Notes: Includes index.
Subjects: Cookery, Moroccan.
Other Authors/Contributors: Clark, Pamela.
Dewey Number: 641.5964

Recipe development Rebecca Squadrito, Nicole Jennings,
Dominic Smith, Elizabeth Macri
Nutritional information Nicole Jennings

Photographers Dean Wilmot, Julie Crespel
Stylist Simon Bajada
Food preparation Sarah Wilmot
Cover Beef and eggplant tagine, page 54

The publishers would like to thank House of Tarek
www.houseoftarek.com.au for props used in photography.

Scanpan cookware is used in the AWW Test Kitchen.

Send recipe enquiries to: recipeenquiries@acpmagazines.com.au